All Colour
Pressure Cooking

Whether you are a newcomer to pressure cooking or whether the cooker is already an established part of your routine, this book will help you make full use of this time-saving and nutritious method of cookery. The variety of foods which can be prepared in a pressure cooker is enormous and there are chapters on stocks, soups, seafood, vegetables, poultry and game, meat, one-pot meals, desserts, preserves and fruit bottling. Each chapter contains a detailed introduction and timetable for pressure cooking that type of food followed by a selection of recipes, every one illustrated in colour. In this edition the final three pages are reserved for you to add your own recipes.

Sue Cutts is Senior Home Economist at The Prestige Group Limited and author of *The Prestige Book of Crockpot Cooking*.

All Colour Pressure Cooking

Sue Cutts

OCTOPUS

Note
All recipes serve 4 people unless otherwise stated
All spoon measures are level
Plain flour and granulated sugar are used unless otherwise stated
All eggs are standard

First published in 1978
by Sundial Books Limited

This edition published in 1981 by
Octopus Books Limited
59 Grosvenor Street
London W1

© Hennerwood Publications Limited

ISBN 0 7064 1676 7

Produced by Mandarin Publishers Limited
22a Westlands Road, Quarry Bay
Hong Kong

Printed in Hong Kong

Contents

Introduction

The majority of foods have to be cooked to make them palatable and digestible. Generally, the higher the temperature they are cooked at, the quicker they cook. In an ordinary saucepan or in the oven, and at normal atmospheric pressure, most liquids will reach boiling point but can get no hotter. As they boil, steam is given off and generally this is lost into the surrounding air.

A pressure cooker, however, is designed to hold in this steam and, with the aid of a pressure weight, builds up to a selected and controlled pressure. The additional pressure increases the temperature of the liquid from $100°C/212°F$ at normal boiling point to $122°C/252°F$ at HIGH (15 lb) pressure. Consequently, foods subjected to this higher temperature will cook more quickly. Additionally, the steam, under pressure, forces its way through the food, softening and tenderizing even the toughest fibres.

Some pressure cookers can be used at three variable pressures, therefore giving three different cooking temperatures. In this way you can select the pressure which will give the best cooking results, just as you would select different temperatures for oven cooking.

Throughout the book, the weights will be referred to as HIGH (15 lb), MEDIUM (10 lb) or LOW (5 lb) and, where applicable, for one design of cooker, a fixed weight of LOW ($7\frac{1}{2}$ lb).

HIGH pressure can be used for the majority of everyday cooking – soups, meat and poultry dishes, vegetables, fish and cereals – and has the advantage of being the fastest method of pressure cooking.

MEDIUM pressure is used for softening fruit for preserves, blanching vegetables prior to home freezing and bottling vegetables.

LOW pressure is used for steamed sweet or savoury puddings and bottling fruit.

How a pressure cooker is made up

There are several different designs of pressure cookers but they all have components which are common to each.

The cooker body and cover

These parts are made of either aluminium or stainless steel and are of a sufficiently high gauge of metal to withstand several times the maximum cooking pressure.

The body of the cooker has a flat, heavy base, making it suitable to use on any form of heat; gas, electricity, radiant, solid or ceramic hotplates, solid

fuel or bottled gas. The latter makes the pressure cooker ideally suited to camping or caravanning, saving numerous saucepans and, of course, fuel.

The body and cover (with gasket) must fit closely together to form an airtight seal. Therefore, it is most important that the rims of both are not dented or damaged in any way. For example, hitting a spoon on the top edge to loosen food from it can make a tiny dent through which steam can escape.

In addition to the airtight seal that is formed between the body and cover, there is also a locking action which ensures that while pressure is inside the cooker, it cannot (and should not) be opened. The locking action will either be in the form of interlocking metal projections on the body and cover or a screw-down metal bar. Both methods ensure that the cooker is correctly closed before use.

The handles

These are made from a heat-resistant material and are either the long saucepan-style handle or the shorter casserole-style. The latter are particularly useful in very confined spaces or where storage is limited.

The gasket

This is one of the most important parts of a pressure cooker as it completes the seal between the body and

cover. The gasket is made from a rubber compound and, as such, does need to be checked and replaced regularly. With constant use, or conversely during prolonged storage between uses, it can harden and will no longer make a good seal.

The pressure weights

All pressure cookers have a pressure control, but it will take differing forms depending on the design of the cooker.

Variable weights
Type A
This weight is made of three screw-together metal bands:
HIGH pressure – all three bands are used together.
MEDIUM pressure – the outer band is removed.
LOW pressure – the outer and middle bands are removed.

In use the bands should be screwed together securely but not so tightly that they cannot be undone with one's fingers. The weight also has a central lifting ring which has a screw fixing.

From left: Type C; Type A; Type B; Type D

In these days of high-speed living a pressure cooker is one of the most useful kitchen aids. Its use is not just confined to cooking vegetables and stews – a whole variety of dishes or cooking processes can be achieved in a fraction of the normal time.

Pressure cookers are extremely reliable and safe and many are manufactured to a British Standard specification. These cookers carry the Kite mark seal of approval, so if you are about to purchase or replace a cooker look out for this symbol. For successful pressure cooking always remember the following safety points:

- Always read and follow the manufacturer's instructions.
- Remember to add the liquid – without it a pressure cooker cannot work.
- Do not attempt to overfill the cooker.
- Time cooking carefully.
- Reduce pressure completely before opening the cooker.

Type B
This weight has a central plunger marked with three rings, each of which corresponds to a pressure. The plunger rises and falls as pressure alters inside the cooker. When only the first ring is visible, LOW pressure has been reached; when two rings are visible, MEDIUM pressure has been reached and when all three are visible, HIGH pressure has been reached.

Both Type A and B weights are positioned by placing them over the centre vent on the cover and pushing down until a slight click is heard. They should not, and do not, require to be screwed on.

Fixed weights
Type C
This weight is screwed into position and has a spring-loaded valve which corresponds to a HIGH pressure only. To build up pressure the lever is moved from a vertical position, downwards, to close the valve.

For those recipes where MEDIUM or LOW pressure is required and for bottling, one manufacturer offers a replacement set of weights converting a fixed weight to a set of three.
Type D
This weight is in the form of a valve which pushes down over a vent in the cover and on reaching LOW pressure ($7\frac{1}{2}$ lb) begins to rotate.

Although this cooker works on a lower pressure, all the cooking times and quantities of liquid in this book may be adjusted so that the recipes may be used.

Adjustments are only required when HIGH or MEDIUM pressure is used for a recipe; the LOW pressure timings and liquid quantities are the same.

As a guide, allow one and a half times the length of cooking time when HIGH pressure is indicated and for those recipes using MEDIUM pressure, refer to the cooking charts or section introduction. Remember to add more liquid for longer cooking times.

Cooking accessories

The trivet

The trivet can either be used in the bottom of the cooker or as a shelf between foods or containers.

Used in the base of the cooker, rim side down, it lifts the foods out of the cooking liquid. In this way the foods are cooked only in steam and a variety can be put together without any fear of the flavour transferring from one type of food to another. The trivet is not used for soups or casseroles where it is essential that the foods and flavours mix.

When bottling it is used with the rim side uppermost and acts as a tray in the bottom of the cooker, preventing the glass bottles from being directly subjected to the base heat.

Separators

These allow several foods to be placed in the cooker, keeping each food separate and making them easier to serve. Separators are either perforated and used for vegetables; solid and used for small cut-up foods, rice, custards, fruit etc.; or in the form of a collapsible basket to use for vegetables.

Some manufacturers offer an optional extra item, such as a large blanching basket. This is most useful for handling larger quantities of vegetables for cooking or blanching.

Safety devices

Pressure cookers are extremely safe appliances, but it cannot be stressed enough that unless the manufacturer's instructions are followed a mishap may occur.

For this reason each pressure cooker has a safety system which works automatically if required. For example, if the centre vent becomes blocked with food, a safety plug will release excess pressure; or if the cooker should boil dry, it may distort the body and cover but the excess heat inside the cooker will cause a fusible metal plug to melt, so releasing the pressure inside. Should either of these occur, turn off the heat and allow the cooker to cool and reduce pressure slowly before opening.

Either, both or a combination of these safety devices is incorporated into each pressure cooker and a more detailed explanation of them will be found in the manufacturer's instruction book.

Basic rules for pressure cooking

Liquids
The liquid used for pressure cooking must be one that gives off steam when it boils, such as milk, water, stock or wine. For this reason, oil or fat should not be used except for pre-frying ingredients before pressure cooking.

So that it is not forgotten, the liquid should always be put in first; the minimum amount to be used will depend on the cooker you own, but generally it is 300 ml/½ pint. This is sufficient for 15 minutes pressure cooking time, but for any additional pressure cooking more liquid must be allowed. As a general rule, a further 150 ml/¼ pint of liquid is required for each additional, or additional part of, 15 minutes cooking time. For example, if a recipe has to be cooked for 45 minutes, 600 ml/1 pint of liquid is required.

Some recipes prove an exception to this rule, such as steamed puddings, where even more liquid is required to allow for some loss during the steaming period, prior to pressure cooking. For these recipes, 750 ml to 1 litre/1¼ to 1¾ pints will be necessary.

Adding boiling water to the cooker is a good short cut and is recommended, particularly for steamed puddings, where the maximum amount of liquid needs to be retained.

Aluminium pressure cookers may discolour if you are living in a hard-water area or when water is boiled in them. (This only applies when the food being cooked is in another container, for example a steamed pudding.) To prevent this discoloration, a little lemon juice or vinegar, approximately 1 × 15 ml spoon/1 tablespoon, should be added to the cooking liquid. Although vinegar is the cheapest to use, it does not have as pleasant an aroma as lemon juice. When freezing lemons, from which you have taken the rind and juice, use the leftovers, cut up, in the cooking water.

Filling levels
All pressure cookers must have sufficient space left in them to allow for the circulation of steam and the expansion of some foods as they cook.

When cooking solid foods, such as a selection of vegetables, the cooker should not be more than two-thirds full. Liquids and high-liquid recipes, such as soups, casseroles, cereal puddings and pasta etc., all tend to boil up inside the cooker. Therefore, for these, the cooker should not be more than half full.

Cooking times
Timing for pressure cooking begins when the cooker has reached pressure and not before. This is usually indicated by a loud hiss or movement of the pressure weight.

Pressure cooking times are often very short and can be quite critical for such foods as vegetables. Therefore, it is a good idea to make use of a kitchen timer with an alarm or the timer you may have on your gas or electric cooker.

So often it is thought that the more food that goes into a pressure cooker, the longer it takes to cook. This is not so. Cooking times are determined by the *size* of the pieces of food. For example; 1.5 kg/3 lb of potatoes will cook in the same time given for 500 g/1 lb. The pieces of food must be the same size if they are to cook evenly; but this is just the same as for ordinary cooking methods. The exception to this rule are joints of meat, or whole poultry which are timed per 500 g/1 lb. The liquid is adjusted accordingly as the cooking times will be longer, see notes on Liquids, left.

Reducing pressure
At the completion of cooking, the pressure inside the cooker *must* be reduced before the cooker is opened. For the majority of cookers there is a locking mechanism which prevents you from being able to open the cooker while the pressure is still maintained.

Pressure is fully reduced in the cooker when the hissing has completely stopped. With all models except Type C where the weight is fixed, the weight should be lifted off before the lid is removed.

Each manufacturer will recommend the methods that may be used for their cookers. However, the methods will fall into two categories – reducing pressure quickly or slowly.

Reducing pressure quickly
This is generally achieved by standing the cooker in a bowl of cold water or running cold water over the side; or for the Type D weight the valve is lifted on to a notch on the air vent.

Reducing pressure slowly
This is always at room temperature, away from the source of heat. This will take at least 10 minutes for most recipes.

The majority of foods can, and should, have pressure reduced quickly to prevent them overcooking, but some *must* have pressure reduced slowly to ensure satisfactory results. These are:

a) High-liquid foods such as soups, or foods which tend to boil and froth up during cooking, such as dried vegetables. For these a quick reduction in pressure could cause the cooking liquid to spurt out of the centre vent and burst the skin on the beans.

b) Milk-based puddings where the sudden drop in pressure could cause curdling and will cause the contents to spurt out of the centre vent.

c) Puddings containing raising agents. Reducing pressure slowly completes the cooking process and therefore, a quick reduction in pressure may cause the pudding to sink. However, this can be overcome by longer pressure cooking times, approximately 10 to 15 minutes at LOW pressure, for a sponge pudding, for example.

d) Bottling. Reducing pressure quickly will cause the bottles to crack and processing will be incomplete.

Cooking a variety of foods together

Unless you are cooking a dish such as a stew, where you want the flavours to mix, the majority of foods will cook only in steam.

Therefore, it is possible to cook together quite different foods, such as fish and meat, without fear of the flavours mixing. This can be particularly convenient if you have a young family; perhaps the baby will be eating a piece of fish the day you are giving the rest of the family a lamb casserole. Remember to allow for the short cooking time of the fish. Reduce the pressure on the casserole, approximately 4 minutes before the end of the time allocated to cook the casserole. Add the fish on a greased trivet, bring back to pressure and complete the cooking time. Alternatively, you may wish to cook a variety of food for your baby. In this way, the very small amounts are not inconvenient to make and you save a little more fuel.

Ingredients for complete courses of a meal can be cooked simultaneously if their cooking times are the same. For example, liver and bacon will cook in the same time as potatoes and a green vegetable. See recipe on page 114.

However, sometimes you will be cooking a larger piece of meat or a casserole and the cooking time will, therefore, be too long to put vegetables in at the beginning. In this case, the vegetables should be added towards the end of the cooking time. For example, for a pot roast of beef served with boiled potatoes and green beans, the cooker has pressure reduced 5 minutes before the end of the time allocated to cook the beef, the vegetables are added, the cooker brought back to pressure and the cooking time completed. See recipe on page 110.

How to use a pressure cooker

All manufacturers provide an instruction book which accompanies each model. These instructions are specifically compiled for each cooker and should be followed with regard to methods of bringing to pressure and reducing pressure after cooking.

The recipes in this book may be used with any model of cooker but some adjustment of ingredients may be necessary to suit the size of your own cooker. See note on filling levels on page 11. If using Type C or Type D cooker, see also pages 9 and 10.

Basic method for use – all models

1. Read the recipe you intend to follow:
a) if there is pre-frying of the ingredients before pressure cooking, this can be done in the open cooker.
b) if you are cooking a joint and it varies in size from that given in the recipe, check that you have the correct amount of liquid to last the cooking time.

2. Where possible put the liquid in first so that it is not forgotten. It should never be less than 300 ml/½ pint. If hot stock is added to prefried ingredients always stir well so the foods are thoroughly mixed and residues from frying are removed from the base.

3. When the ingredients and seasoning have been added, close the cooker by locking on the cover correctly and securely.

4. Unless the recipe states otherwise, bring to pressure on a high heat. The appropriate weight should always be placed over the vent unless steaming is included in the recipe.

Type A weight: Put the weight on to the centre vent as soon as the cover has been closed. (This is a revised method of use recommended by the manufacturer.) Wait until there is a loud hiss and escape of steam around the weight. Begin timing and reduce the heat so that the cooker is hissing gently and there is only a slight escape of steam around the weight.

Type B weight: Put the weight on to the centre vent as soon as the cover has been closed. After a few moments steam will escape from the air vent before the plunger rises to close it. The plunger in the indicator weight will then begin to rise. Wait until the required pressure is reached, indicated by the number of rings showing (all three for HIGH pressure). Begin timing and reduce the heat so that the pressure remains constant.

Type C weight: The valve weight is always screwed into position on the cover. The valve lever should be in the upright position when the cover is closed. Wait until there is a steady flow of steam from the valve before lowering the lever, then wait until pressure is reached, indicated by a loud hiss and escape of steam around the valve. Begin timing and reduce the heat so that the cooker is hissing gently and there is only a slight escape of steam around the valve.

Type D weight: Put the valve into position over the vent. Wait until the valve begins to rotate and there is an escape of steam around it. Begin timing and reduce the heat so that the valve remains steady and there is an occasional escape of steam.

5. After bringing the cooker to high, medium or low pressure, reduce the heat and maintain the pressure, over a steady, slow heat.

6. Reduce pressure quickly or slowly as recommended in the recipe. Always reduce pressure completely before attempting to remove the cover.

Type A, B, C weight cookers – Reducing pressure quickly: Stand the cooker in a bowl of cold water, or run cold water over the cover and sides.

Type D weight cooker – Reducing pressure quickly: Lift the valve slightly on to the notch on the vent and allow the steam to escape.

All cookers – Reducing pressure slowly: Move the cooker away from the source of heat and allow the pressure to drop at room temperature. This will take 10 to 15 minutes for most recipes.

Care of a pressure cooker

Before the first use and after subsequent uses, the cooker should be washed in hot soapy water, rinsed and dried thoroughly. Washing soda should not be used as it can damage aluminium cookers. The cover and gasket do not necessarily require washing after each use, usually a wipe with a damp cloth is sufficient. The gasket should not be washed too often in detergents, as with all rubber materials this may cause it to perish.

Check the centre vent frequently to ensure that it is not becoming blocked. If a blockage does occur, it can usually be removed with a washing-up brush, pipe cleaner or skewer. Non-stick linings are available on some pressure cookers and are extremely useful, particularly when making milk puddings, jam or pre-frying meats for casseroles etc. However, like all non-stick surfaces, these should be treated with care and abrasives or abrasive cloths should not be used on them. Soap-filled steel wool or nylon scouring pads may be used on the inside of the cooker (except Teflon non-stick coatings) but should not be used on the outside, as the highly polished finish may become damaged. Similarly, with those pressure cookers which have attractive coloured enamelled paint finishes on the outside abrasive cleaners should be avoided, otherwise the surface will become scratched.

The discoloration that may occur on the inside of your cooker is not dangerous. It generally occurs on aluminium utensils in hard water areas and can be prevented by adding an acid to the cooking liquid. See Liquids, on page 11. To remove the discoloration, clean with a soap-filled steel wool pad or simmer a strong solution of cream of tartar or vinegar in the cooker. Alternatively, wait until you are cooking fruit when either the fruit itself will clean the cooker or in the case of apples, the peelings, boiled in water for a few minutes, will remove the black markings.

Most pressure cookers can be washed in a dishwasher, although the gasket should be removed before doing so. To prevent water staining or dulling the highly polished finishes, it is good practice to take the cooker out of the machine as soon as the cycle is completed.

When storing the cooker ensure that air can circulate freely through it. Otherwise, if left tightly closed the cooker may become musty between uses, particularly if it is left for some months.

For most cookers the lid can be placed upside down on the body, except for the fixed weight cookers that have a clamp fixing which, if inverted, could become lodged under the lugs. For these, sit the cover loosely on top of the body.

All manufacturers make spare parts, such as gaskets and safety plugs, and these should be checked at least once a year to ensure that they are in good working order.

Repair and reconditioning will also be undertaken by reputable manufacturers, so that your pressure cooker can give you many efficient and happy years of service.

Stocks and Soups

The basis for many well-flavoured recipes is a good stock. Many of the recipes in this book use stock and, while the commercial bouillon or stock cubes are an excellent standby, the flavour of the homemade variety is much more individual.

Stocks are inexpensive to make as often they use up bones, carcasses and vegetables that would otherwise be discarded. However, it is not a good idea to use really old and sad vegetables or equally those that will produce strong flavours, such as turnips or swedes. Turnips or swedes with potatoes, should be used sparingly as they can make the stock cloudy and reduce its keeping qualities.

Chicken, turkey or game carcasses, cooked or uncooked, make excellent stocks for use with all poultry dishes. The flavour of the dish is, of course, enhanced if it is prepared with its own type of stock, e.g. fish stock for fish dishes, etc.

If you own a home freezer the bones that are a by-product of the meat you buy, and for which you have probably paid, can be put to good use in making brown or white stock which can then be frozen. Ask the butcher to chop the bones for you, as smaller pieces give more flavour. Fish stock is really only worth making on the day you intend to use it, as it does not keep.

Stocks can be frozen most successfully either in ice-cube trays or in convenient amounts for recipes. A pressure-cooked stock is concentrated, so it takes up less space in storage. Before freezing, or storing in the refrigerator, the stock should be thoroughly cooled and the layer of fat removed. Stock stored in a refrigerator will keep for 3–4 days; in a home freezer for six months.

Soups

The true value of a pressure cooker is seen when making dishes that would normally take one or more hours to cook. Homemade soups fall into this category, but with the aid of your pressure cooker you can reduce an hour to a matter of minutes. Soups do not necessarily have to be confined to cold winter days – a chilled soup on a hot summer's day can be very refreshing and a little different, particularly for a special occasion.

Soups freeze very well, but because the pressure cooker should never be more than half full, it is important to note that if you wish to make large quantities it may be necessary to cook two or three batches. Alternatively, make a very concentrated recipe and dilute afterwards. The latter method is advantageous for the freezer as less storage space is required, and by using the method given below for re-heating you will probably achieve the consistency you require.

General rules for making soups

1. HIGH pressure can be used for all soups.
2. The trivet is not required.
3. If vegetables or meats are to be prefried, this can be done in the open cooker over a low heat.
4. THE COOKER MUST NEVER BE MORE THAN HALF FULL WHEN ALL THE INGREDIENTS AND LIQUID HAVE BEEN ADDED.
5. Season lightly for cooking. Foods retain more concentrated flavours during pressure cooking and it is always desirable to taste and adjust the seasoning just before serving.
6. Pressure can be reduced quickly for all soups, with the exception of those containing dried pulses such as lentils or haricot beans. For these soups, reduce pressure slowly as this will prevent the skins of the pulses splitting.
7. Thickening should be done in the open cooker, after pressure cooking. Blended cornflour, blended flour, cream or egg yolks may be used. If thickening with cream or egg yolks, first beat the egg yolks with a fork to combine. Add a little of the hot soup to the cream or egg yolks and stir to combine. Gradually stir the mixture into the hot soup. To prevent curdling the soup should not be boiled after the cream or egg yolks have been added.

Reheating frozen soups

Put 150 ml/¼ pint water into the cooker with the block of soup, turned out of its freezer wrappings or container. Close the cooker and bring to HIGH pressure. Cook for 5 minutes. Reduce pressure quickly. Adjust consistency and seasoning.

Brown stock

METRIC	IMPERIAL
50 g lard or dripping	*2 oz lard or dripping*
1 kg bones, cooked or uncooked, chopped	*2 lb bones, cooked or uncooked, chopped*
1 onion, peeled and sliced	*1 onion, peeled and sliced*
1 carrot, scraped and sliced	*1 carrot, scraped and sliced*
2 stalks celery, scrubbed and chopped	*2 stalks celery, scrubbed and chopped*
approx. 900 ml water	*approx. 1½ pints water*
a little salt	*a little salt*
freshly ground black pepper	*freshly ground black pepper*
1 bay leaf	*1 bay leaf*

H Pressure – 30 to 45 minutes

METHOD

Heat the lard or dripping in the cooker and brown the bones and vegetables well. Add the water and make sure that the cooker is not more than half full. Bring to the boil and skim thoroughly, add the salt, pepper and bay leaf. Close the cooker and bring to H pressure. Cook uncooked bones for 45 minutes, cooked bones for 30 minutes. Reduce pressure quickly. Strain and cool thoroughly and remove fat before using.

Chilled cucumber soup

METRIC	IMPERIAL
25 g butter or margarine	*1 oz butter or margarine*
1 small onion, peeled and coarsely chopped	*1 small onion, peeled and coarsely chopped*
2 cucumbers, peeled, seeded and coarsely chopped	*2 cucumbers, peeled, seeded and coarsely chopped*
900 ml white stock or water and 1 chicken stock cube	*1½ pints white stock or water and 1 chicken stock cube*
salt	*salt*
white pepper	*white pepper*
a little milk (optional)	*a little milk (optional)*
To finish:	**To finish:**
150 ml single cream	*¼ pint single cream*
a few drops of green food colouring	*a few drops of green food colouring*
a little freshly chopped mint to garnish	*a little freshly chopped mint to garnish*

H Pressure – 5 minutes

METHOD

Heat the butter or margarine in the cooker and fry the onion and cucumbers for a few minutes, without colouring. Add the stock or water and stock cube and a little salt and pepper. Make sure that the cooker is not more than half full. Close the cooker, bring to H pressure and cook for 5 minutes. Reduce the pressure quickly. Blend the soup in a liquidizer or press through a sieve. Add a little milk if the consistency requires thinning; the soup should be the consistency of single cream. Cool and chill thoroughly in the refrigerator. Stir in the cream, taste and adjust the seasoning as necessary. Before serving stir in a few drops of green food colouring. Garnish with chopped mint.

White or poultry stock

When white or poultry stock are used in recipes, remember that uncooked bones produce white stock and poultry carcasses, such as chicken or turkey, produce poultry stock.

METRIC	IMPERIAL
1 kg uncooked bones or poultry carcasses	*2 lb uncooked bones or poultry carcasses*
1 onion, peeled and sliced	*1 onion, peeled and sliced*
2 stalks celery, scrubbed and chopped	*2 stalks celery, scrubbed and chopped*
approx. 900 ml water	*approx. 1½ pints water*
a little salt	*a little salt*
freshly ground black pepper	*freshly ground black pepper*
1 bay leaf	*1 bay leaf*

H Pressure – 30 to 45 minutes

METHOD

Place bones or carcasses, onion, celery and water in the cooker. Make sure that the cooker is not more than half full. Bring to the boil and skim thoroughly. Add the salt, pepper and bay leaf. Close the cooker and bring to H pressure. Cook uncooked bones for 45 minutes and carcasses for 30 minutes. Reduce pressure quickly. Strain and cool thoroughly and remove fat before using.

Corn soup

METRIC	IMPERIAL
25 g butter or margarine	*1 oz butter or margarine*
1 onion, peeled and chopped	*1 onion, peeled and chopped*
2 potatoes, peeled and diced	*2 potatoes, peeled and diced*
500 g sweetcorn kernels, (frozen or canned)	*1 lb sweetcorn kernels, (frozen or canned)*
900 ml white stock or water and 1 chicken stock cube	*1½ pints white stock or water and 1 chicken stock cube*
salt	*salt*
freshly ground black pepper	*freshly ground black pepper*
1 × 1.25 ml spoon ground nutmeg	*¼ teaspoon ground nutmeg*
To finish:	**To finish:**
1 × 15 ml spoon flour	*1 tablespoon flour*
150 ml milk	*¼ pint milk*
a little finely chopped green pepper	*a little finely chopped green pepper*

H Pressure – 8 minutes

METHOD

Heat the butter or margarine in the cooker and lightly fry the onion and potatoes. Stir in the sweetcorn, stock or water and stock cube, salt and pepper and nutmeg. Close the cooker, bring to H pressure and cook for 8 minutes. Reduce the pressure quickly. Blend the soup in a liquidizer or press through a sieve. Return the soup to the open cooker. Blend the flour with the milk, add to the soup and bring to the boil, stirring constantly. Taste and adjust the seasoning as necessary before serving. Garnish with a little green pepper.

Fish stock

METRIC
500–750 g fish bones and
  trimmings
1 small onion, peeled and
  sliced
1 stalk celery, scrubbed and
  chopped
approx. 600–900 ml water
a few white peppercorns
1 blade mace
a little salt

IMPERIAL
1–1½ lb fish bones and
  trimmings
1 small onion, peeled and
  sliced
1 stalk celery, scrubbed and
  chopped
approx. 1–1½ pints water
a few white peppercorns
1 blade mace
a little salt

H Pressure – 15 minutes

METHOD
Place fish bones and trimmings, onion, celery and water in
the cooker. Make sure that the cooker is not more than half
full. Bring to the boil and skim thoroughly. Add the peppercorns, mace and salt. Close the cooker and bring to pressure. Cook for 15 minutes. Reduce pressure quickly. Strain
and cool thoroughly before using.

Corn soup ; Chilled cucumber soup

Celery soup

METRIC
1 large head celery, scrubbed
  and coarsely chopped
  (reserve a few leaves to chop
  for garnish)
1 onion, peeled and coarsely
  chopped
900 ml white stock or water
  and 1 chicken stock cube
salt
freshly ground black pepper
1 bay leaf
To finish:
2 × 5 ml spoons cornflour
150 ml milk

IMPERIAL
1 large head celery, scrubbed
  and coarsely chopped
  (reserve a few leaves to chop
  for garnish)
1 onion, peeled and coarsely
  chopped
1½ pints white stock or water
  and 1 chicken stock cube
salt
freshly ground black pepper
1 bay leaf
To finish:
2 teaspoons cornflour
¼ pint milk

H Pressure – 12 minutes

METHOD
Put all the ingredients, except the cornflour and milk, into
the cooker. Make sure that the cooker is not more than half
full. Close the cooker and bring to H pressure. Cook for 12
minutes. Reduce pressure quickly. Remove bay leaf. Blend
soup in a liquidizer or press through a sieve. Return to the
open cooker to reheat. Blend the cornflour with the milk.

Stir into the soup to thicken, bring to the boil, taste and
adjust the seasoning as necessary. Serve garnished with
reserved chopped celery leaves.

Cream of mushroom soup

METRIC
500 g mushrooms, cleaned
  and thinly sliced (reserve a
  few slices for garnish)
1 small onion, finely chopped
900 ml white stock or water
  and 1 chicken stock cube
1 bay leaf
salt
freshly ground black pepper
To finish:
1 × 15 ml spoon cornflour
2 × 15 ml spoons water
150 ml single cream

IMPERIAL
1 lb mushrooms, cleaned and
  thinly sliced (reserve a few
  slices for garnish)
1 small onion, finely chopped
1½ pints white stock or water
  and 1 chicken stock cube
1 bay leaf
salt
freshly ground black pepper
To finish:
1 tablespoon cornflour
2 tablespoons water
¼ pint single cream

H Pressure – 5 minutes

METHOD
Put the mushrooms into the cooker and add the onion, stock
or water and stock cube, bay leaf and a little salt and pepper.
Make sure that the cooker is not more than half full. Close

From left: Celery soup; Cream of mushroom soup; Cream of onion soup; Cream of artichoke soup

H Pressure – 5 minutes

METHOD

Heat the butter or margarine in the cooker, fry the onions gently, without colouring, until they start to soften. Add the stock or water and stock cube and a little salt and pepper. Make sure that the cooker is not more than half full. Close the cooker, bring to H pressure and cook for 5 minutes. Reduce the pressure quickly. Blend soup in a liquidizer or press through a sieve. Return the soup to the open cooker. Blend the flour with the milk, add to the soup and bring to the boil, stirring constantly. Stir in the cream just before serving and taste and adjust the seasoning as necessary. Garnish with chopped chives.

Cream of artichoke soup

METRIC	IMPERIAL
750 g Jerusalem artichokes	1½ lb Jerusalem artichokes
cold water	cold water
juice of 1 lemon	juice of 1 lemon
50 g butter or margarine	2 oz butter or margarine
1 small onion, peeled and chopped	1 small onion, peeled and chopped
900 ml white stock or water and 1 chicken stock cube	1½ pints white stock or water and 1 chicken stock cube
1 bay leaf	1 bay leaf
a few parsley stalks	a few parsley stalks
salt	salt
freshly ground black pepper	freshly ground black pepper
To finish:	**To finish:**
150 ml single cream	¼ pint single cream
a little finely chopped fresh parsley	a little finely chopped fresh parsley

H Pressure – 6 minutes

METHOD

Peel the artichokes and cut into 2.5 cm/1 inch pieces. Place in cold water to cover and add the strained lemon juice to prevent discoloration. Heat the butter or margarine in the cooker and fry the onion until transparent. Drain and dry the artichokes then add to the cooker. Sauté for a few minutes, without colouring. Add the stock or water and stock cube, bay leaf, parsley stalks and a little salt and pepper to the cooker. Close the cooker, bring to H pressure and cook for 6 minutes. Reduce pressure quickly and remove the bay leaf. Blend the soup in a liquidizer or press through a sieve.

To serve hot: return the soup to the open cooker and reheat, adjusting the seasoning if necessary. Stir in the cream just before serving and garnish with a little chopped parsley.

To serve chilled: after liquidizing, cool the soup and chill thoroughly in the refrigerator. Before serving, adjust the seasoning if necessary and stir in the cream. Garnish with a little chopped parsley.

the cooker and bring to H pressure, cook for 5 minutes. Reduce the pressure quickly and remove the bay leaf. Blend the soup in a liquidizer or if preferred, leave the soup as it is. Return the soup to the open cooker, stir in the cornflour blended with the water. Reheat, stirring constantly, until boiling and thickened. Just before serving, stir in the cream, taste and adjust the seasoning as necessary and garnish with slices of raw mushroom.

Cream of onion soup

METRIC	IMPERIAL
25 g butter or margarine	1 oz butter or margarine
500 g onions, peeled and thinly sliced	1 lb onions, peeled and thinly sliced
900 ml white stock or water and 1 chicken stock cube	1½ pints white stock or water and 1 chicken stock cube
salt	salt
freshly ground black pepper	freshly ground black pepper
To finish:	**To finish:**
1 × 15 ml spoon flour	1 tablespoon flour
150 ml milk	¼ pint milk
2 × 15 ml spoons single cream	2 tablespoons single cream
freshly chopped chives to garnish	freshly chopped chives to garnish

Tomato and orange soup

METRIC	IMPERIAL
25 g butter or margarine	1 oz butter or margarine
1 onion, peeled and finely chopped	1 onion, peeled and finely chopped
2 small carrots, scraped and thinly sliced	2 small carrots, scraped and thinly sliced
1 large potato, peeled and cut into small dice	1 large potato, peeled and cut into small dice
750 g tomatoes, quartered	1½ lb tomatoes, quartered
finely grated rind and juice of 2 oranges	finely grated rind and juice of 2 oranges
1 bay leaf	1 bay leaf
600 ml white stock or water and ½ chicken stock cube	1 pint white stock or water and ½ chicken stock cube
salt	salt
freshly ground black pepper	freshly ground black pepper
1 × 5 ml spoon caster sugar	1 teaspoon caster sugar
To finish:	**To finish:**
1 × 15 ml spoon flour	1 tablespoon flour
150 ml milk	¼ pint milk
2 × 15 ml spoons single cream	2 tablespoons single cream

H Pressure – 5 minutes

METHOD

Heat the butter or margarine in the cooker and fry the onion, carrots, and potato without colouring. Add the tomatoes, grated rind of 1 orange and the juice of 2 oranges, the bay leaf, stock or water and stock cube, salt, pepper and sugar. Make sure that the cooker is not more than half full. Close the cooker, bring to H pressure and cook for 5 minutes. Reduce the pressure quickly. Blend soup in a liquidizer or press through a sieve and return to the open cooker. Blend the flour with the milk and stir into the soup. Return to the heat and cook, stirring constantly, until boiling and thickened. Taste and adjust the seasoning as necessary. Just before serving pour into a heated tureen, pour the cream in a swirl over the centre and sprinkle with the remaining orange rind.

Tomato and orange soup; Minestrone; Lentil and tomato soup

Minestrone

Minestrone can be made with almost any variety of vegetables. This version has haricot beans added, making it more substantial.

METRIC	IMPERIAL
100 g small haricot beans	4 oz small haricot beans
cold water	cold water
25 g lard or dripping	1 oz lard or dripping
1 thick rasher unsmoked bacon, rinded and chopped	1 thick rasher unsmoked bacon, rinded and chopped
1 onion, peeled and chopped	1 onion, peeled and chopped
1 clove garlic, crushed	1 clove garlic, crushed
2 carrots, scraped and sliced	2 carrots, scraped and sliced
2 stalks celery, scrubbed and chopped	2 stalks celery, scrubbed and chopped
225 g tomatoes, skinned and chopped	8 oz tomatoes, skinned and chopped
2 × 15 ml spoons tomato purée	2 tablespoons tomato purée
900 ml white stock or water and 1 chicken stock cube	1½ pints white stock or water and 1 chicken stock cube
salt	salt
freshly ground black pepper	freshly ground black pepper
¼ small, white cabbage, washed and finely shredded	¼ small, white cabbage, washed and finely shredded
2 × 15 ml spoons small pasta shells or rings	2 tablespoons small pasta shells or rings
To finish:	**To finish:**
finely grated Parmesan cheese	finely grated Parmesan cheese

H Pressure – 15 to 20 minutes

METHOD

Cover the haricot beans with cold water and soak overnight or cover with boiling water and soak for 1 hour. Heat the lard or dripping in the cooker, fry the bacon, onion, garlic, carrots and celery until all are lightly coloured. Add the drained haricot beans, tomatoes, tomato purée, stock or water and stock cube, salt and pepper. Make sure that the cooker is not more than half full. Close the cooker and bring to H pressure, cook for 10 minutes. Reduce the pressure slowly. Check the haricot beans for tenderness. If they are still very hard cook for a further 5 minutes at H pressure and reduce pressure slowly. If the haricot beans are almost tender omit this step. Add the cabbage and pasta, stir well. Bring back to H pressure and cook for a further 5 minutes. Reduce the pressure slowly (this will prevent the beans from splitting). Taste and adjust the seasoning as necessary, pour into a heated tureen and serve with Parmesan cheese.

Lentil and tomato soup

METRIC	IMPERIAL
100 g lentils	4 oz lentils
boiling water	boiling water
25 g lard or margarine	1 oz lard or margarine
1 onion, peeled and chopped	1 onion, peeled and chopped
2 rashers bacon, rinded and chopped	2 rashers bacon, rinded and chopped
2 carrots, scraped and sliced	2 carrots, scraped and sliced
500 g tomatoes, skinned and chopped	1 lb tomatoes, skinned and chopped
900 ml white stock or water and 1 chicken stock cube	1½ pints white stock or water and 1 chicken stock cube
1 bay leaf	1 bay leaf
salt	salt
freshly ground black pepper	freshly ground black pepper
a little milk (optional)	a little milk (optional)
toasted bread croûtons	toasted bread croûtons

H Pressure – 15 minutes

METHOD

Cover the lentils with boiling water and leave to soak for 1 hour. Heat the lard or margarine in the cooker and fry the onion, bacon and carrots without browning. Add the drained lentils, tomatoes, stock or water and stock cube, bay leaf and salt and pepper. Close the cooker, bring to H pressure and cook for 15 minutes. Reduce the pressure slowly and remove the bay leaf. Blend the soup in a liquidizer or press through a sieve. Return the soup to the open cooker to reheat. Adjust the consistency with a little milk if necessary. Taste and adjust the seasoning as necessary. Serve with toasted croûtons.

Farmhouse vegetable soup

METRIC	IMPERIAL
2 carrots, peeled and cut into small dice	2 carrots, peeled and cut into small dice
1 swede, peeled and cut into small dice	1 swede, peeled and cut into small dice
1 parsnip, peeled and cut into small dice	1 parsnip, peeled and cut into small dice
2 potatoes, peeled and cut into small dice	2 potatoes, peeled and cut into small dice
1 small onion, peeled and roughly chopped	1 small onion, peeled and roughly chopped
2 small leeks, cleaned and thinly sliced	2 small leeks, cleaned and thinly sliced
1 bay leaf	1 bay leaf
900 ml brown stock or water and 1 beef stock cube	1½ pints brown stock or water and 1 beef stock cube
salt	salt
freshly ground black pepper	freshly ground black pepper

To finish:

beurre manié, made with 25 g butter mixed with 1 × 15 ml spoon flour	beurre manié, made with 1 oz butter mixed with 1 tablespoon flour

H Pressure – 5 minutes

METHOD

Place all the vegetables into the cooker with the bay leaf, stock or water and stock cube and a little salt and pepper. Make sure that the cooker is not more than half full. Close the cooker, bring to H pressure and cook for 5 minutes. Reduce the pressure quickly. Remove the bay leaf, return the open cooker to the heat and add the beurre manié in small pieces, stirring constantly. Cook until thickened. Taste and adjust the seasoning as necessary before serving.

Seafood chowder

METRIC	IMPERIAL
4 rashers unsmoked streaky bacon, rinded and chopped	4 rashers unsmoked streaky bacon, rinded and chopped
1 onion, peeled and coarsely chopped	1 onion, peeled and coarsely chopped
1 large potato, peeled and cut into 1 cm cubes	1 large potato, peeled and cut into ½ inch cubes
500 g cod or fresh haddock fillets, cut into 2.5 cm cubes	1 lb cod or fresh haddock fillets, cut into 1 inch cubes
600 ml fish stock or water and ½ chicken stock cube	1 pint fish stock or water and ½ chicken stock cube
1 bay leaf	1 bay leaf
a pinch of powdered mace	a pinch of powdered mace
salt	salt
freshly ground black pepper	freshly ground black pepper

To finish:

1 × 15 ml spoon flour	1 tablespoon flour
150 ml milk	¼ pint milk
50 g shelled prawns	2 oz shelled prawns
75 g cooked mussels	3 oz cooked mussels
freshly chopped chives to garnish	freshly chopped chives to garnish

Split pea and bacon soup

METRIC	IMPERIAL
100 g unsmoked streaky bacon, rinded and chopped	*4 oz unsmoked streaky bacon, rinded and chopped*
25 g butter or margarine	*1 oz butter or margarine*
1 large onion, peeled and chopped	*1 large onion, peeled and chopped*
100 g split peas	*4 oz split peas*
900 ml white stock or water and 1 chicken stock cube	*1½ pints white stock or water and 1 chicken stock cube*
salt	*salt*
freshly ground black pepper	*freshly ground black pepper*

H Pressure – 12 minutes

METHOD
Heat the cooker gently, add the bacon and fry in its own fat until softened. Add the butter or margarine and fry the onion without colouring. Add the split peas, stock or water and stock cube and a little salt and pepper. Close the cooker, bring to H pressure and cook for 12 minutes. Reduce the pressure slowly. Blend the soup in a liquidizer or press through a sieve. Return to the open cooker to reheat. Taste and adjust the seasoning as necessary before serving.

Scotch broth

METRIC	IMPERIAL
500 g scrag or middle neck of lamb, cut into thin chops and trimmed of fat	*1 lb scrag or middle neck of lamb, cut into thin chops and trimmed of fat*
25 g pearl barley, washed	*1 oz pearl barley, washed*
2 carrots, scraped and diced	*2 carrots, scraped and diced*
1 onion, peeled and chopped	*1 onion, peeled and chopped*
2 small leeks, washed and thinly sliced	*2 small leeks, washed and thinly sliced*
900 ml white stock or water and 1 chicken stock cube	*1½ pints white stock or water and 1 chicken stock cube*
salt	*salt*
freshly ground black pepper	*freshly ground black pepper*
a little freshly chopped parsley, to garnish	*a little freshly chopped parsley, to garnish*

H Pressure – 10 minutes

METHOD
Put all the ingredients, except the parsley, into the cooker. Make sure that the cooker is not more than half full. Bring to the boil in the open cooker and skim well. Close the cooker and bring to H pressure, cook for 10 minutes. Reduce the pressure slowly. Lift out the meat and remove from the bones. Chop the meat into small pieces and return it to the broth. Reheat in the open cooker, taste and adjust the seasoning as necessary. Garnish with the chopped parsley before serving.

H Pressure – 3 minutes

METHOD
Heat the cooker, add the bacon and fry lightly in its own fat. Add the onion and potato, fry until lightly coloured. Remove from the cooker and drain well. If necessary, add a little fat to the cooker to fry the fish and cook until beginning to colour. Carefully drain off the fat before adding the stock or water and stock cube, bay leaf, mace, salt, pepper and vegetable mixture. Make sure that the cooker is not more than half full. Close the cooker and bring to H pressure, cook for 3 minutes. Reduce the pressure quickly. Blend the flour with the milk and stir into the chowder, off the heat, with the prawns and mussels. Return to the heat and bring to the boil, stirring constantly. Taste and adjust the seasoning as necessary. Pour into a heated tureen and garnish with the chopped chives.

Served with French bread this is a meal in itself.

Red bean and pepper soup

METRIC	IMPERIAL
100 g small red kidney beans	4 oz small red kidney beans
900 ml white stock or water and 1 chicken stock cube	1½ pints white stock or water and 1 chicken stock cube
2 rashers unsmoked streaky bacon, rinded and chopped	2 rashers unsmoked streaky bacon, rinded and chopped
1 small onion, peeled and coarsely chopped	1 small onion, peeled and coarsely chopped
2 red peppers, cored, seeded and chopped	2 red peppers, cored, seeded and chopped
4 tomatoes, skinned and quartered	4 tomatoes, skinned and quartered
salt	salt
freshly ground black pepper	freshly ground black pepper
1 bay leaf	1 bay leaf

H Pressure – 15 minutes

METHOD

Put the beans into a basin. Bring 450 ml/¾ pint of the stock or water to the boil, pour over the beans to cover and leave to stand for 1 hour. Heat the cooker gently and fry the bacon in its own fat. Add a little more fat if necessary and fry the onion and peppers, without colouring. Add the tomatoes, beans with their soaking liquid, the remaining stock or water and stock cube, salt, pepper and bay leaf. Close the cooker, bring to H pressure and cook for 15 minutes. Reduce the pressure slowly. Remove the bay leaf and blend the soup in a liquidizer or press through a sieve. Return to the open cooker to reheat, taste and adjust the seasoning as necessary.

Chicken noodle soup

METRIC	IMPERIAL
1 chicken portion, skinned	1 chicken portion, skinned
1 small onion, peeled and chopped	1 small onion, peeled and chopped
1 carrot, cut into small dice	1 carrot, cut into small dice
50 g fine noodles, such as vermicelli or egg noodles	2 oz fine noodles, such as vermicelli or egg noodles
1 × 2.5 ml spoon dried thyme	½ teaspoon dried thyme
900 ml poultry stock or water and 1 chicken stock cube	1½ pints poultry stock or water and 1 chicken stock cube
salt	salt
freshly ground black pepper	freshly ground black pepper
a little fresh parsley, chopped, to garnish	a little fresh parsley, chopped, to garnish

H Pressure – 4 minutes

METHOD

If using a leg portion of chicken, cut into 2 pieces – thigh and drumstick. Place the chicken, vegetables, noodles, thyme, stock or water and stock cube and a little salt and pepper into the cooker. Make sure that the cooker is not more than half full. Close the cooker, bring to H pressure and cook for 4 minutes. Reduce the pressure quickly. Lift out the chicken and remove the meat from the bones. Cut the meat into small pieces and return to the soup. Reheat the soup and taste and adjust the seasoning as necessary. Serve garnished with chopped parsley.

Cock-a-leekie soup

Above: Cock-a-leekie soup; Left: Red bean and pepper soup; Chicken noodle soup

METRIC
1 small boiling fowl (approx.
  1.5 kg), cleaned and trussed
1 bouquet garni
salt
freshly ground black pepper
1.2 litres water
4 large leeks, washed, sliced
  lengthways and cut into
  2.5 cm pieces
8 prunes, soaked for 10
  minutes in boiling water,
  then drained, stoned and
  halved

IMPERIAL
1 small boiling fowl (approx.
  3 lb), cleaned and trussed
1 bouquet garni
salt
freshly ground black pepper
2 pints water
4 large leeks, washed, sliced
  lengthways and cut into
  1 inch pieces
8 prunes, soaked for 10
  minutes in boiling water,
  then drained, stoned and
  halved

A whole boiling fowl will produce more than sufficient meat for the soup. However, the leftover meat can be used for another dish, e.g. chicken pie, see page 59.

H Pressure – 30 minutes

METHOD
Put the fowl, bouquet garni, salt, pepper and water into the cooker. Bring to the boil and skim well. Make sure that the cooker is not more than half full. Close the cooker, bring to H pressure and cook for 20 minutes. Reduce the pressure quickly. Add the leeks and prunes. Bring back to H pressure and cook for a further 10 minutes. Reduce the pressure quickly. Lift out the fowl, remove the skin and discard. Cut some of the flesh into large pieces and return to the soup to reheat. Remove the bouquet garni and taste and adjust the seasoning, as necessary, before serving.

Mulligatawny

METRIC

25 g dripping or lard

500 g lean scrag of mutton or lamb, cut into thin chops

1 large onion, peeled and sliced

1 large carrot, scraped and sliced

1 large cooking apple, peeled, cored and chopped

2 × 5 ml spoons curry powder

a generous pinch of chilli powder

1.2 litres white stock or water and 1 chicken stock cube

a little salt

To finish:

1 × 15 ml spoon flour

150 ml milk

a little finely chopped green pepper, to garnish

H Pressure – 15 minutes

IMPERIAL

1 oz dripping or lard

1 lb lean scrag of mutton or lamb, cut into thin chops

1 large onion, peeled and sliced

1 large carrot, scraped and sliced

1 large cooking apple, peeled, cored and chopped

2 teaspoons curry powder

a generous pinch of chilli powder

2 pints white stock or water and 1 chicken stock cube

a little salt

To finish:

1 tablespoon flour

$\frac{1}{4}$ pint milk

a little finely chopped green pepper, to garnish

METHOD

Heat the dripping or lard in the cooker, brown the meat, vegetables and apple. Stir in the curry and chilli powders and cook for a few minutes. Add the stock or water and stock cube with a little salt and stir well. Make sure that the cooker is not more than half full. Close the cooker, bring to H pressure and cook for 15 minutes. Reduce the pressure quickly. Remove the meat from the bones, cut into small pieces and set aside. Blend the vegetables and stock in a liquidizer or press through a sieve. Return the soup to the cooker, stir in the flour blended with the milk and bring to the boil, stirring constantly. Put the meat back into the soup to reheat. Taste and adjust the seasoning as necessary. Garnish with chopped green pepper.

This soup is also delicious served cold. The consistency may need to be thinner as it thickens when chilled. Cover the surface of the soup with a piece of damp greaseproof paper or foil to prevent a skin from forming.

Beef and onion soup

METRIC

25 g lard or margarine
2 large onions, peeled and
  coarsely chopped
225 g minced beef
900 ml brown stock or water
  and 1 beef stock cube
1 × 5 ml spoon
  Worcestershire sauce
salt
freshly ground black pepper

To finish:

25 g butter or margarine
1 onion, peeled and thinly
  sliced
a little fresh parsley, chopped

H Pressure – 8 minutes

IMPERIAL

1 oz lard or margarine
2 large onions, peeled and
  coarsely chopped
8 oz minced beef
1½ pints brown stock or water
  and 1 beef stock cube
1 teaspoon Worcestershire
  sauce
salt
freshly ground black pepper

To finish:

1 oz butter or margarine
1 onion, peeled and thinly
  sliced
a little fresh parsley, chopped

METHOD

Heat the lard or margarine in the cooker and fry the onions until they start to colour. Lift the onions out, set aside and brown the meat. Add the stock or water and stock cube, Worcestershire sauce, salt, pepper and fried onion, stir well. Make sure that the cooker is not more than half full. Close the cooker and bring to H pressure, cook for 8 minutes. Reduce the pressure quickly. Blend soup in a liquidizer or press through a sieve. Return to the open cooker to reheat. Taste and adjust the seasoning as necessary. Heat the butter or margarine in a frying pan and fry the onion briskly until well browned. Transfer the soup to a heated tureen and garnish with the onion rings and chopped parsley.

Mulligatawny; Beef and onion soup

Seafoods

Fish are very valuable to our diet. Not only do they add variety to the many other protein foods we require daily, but they also contain valuable sources of other nutrients – such as vitamins and minerals.

In a pressure cooker, most fish are cooked very quickly – in five minutes or less – therefore they lend themselves to being cooked with their accompanying vegetables. And because everything is cooked in steam, the fishy flavour will not impregnate the potatoes, beans etc. that are added. Another benefit is that most of the fishy cooking smell will be contained inside the cooker, so you will not feel that you have eaten the meal before you begin!

Fish can be either poached or steamed, or if you wish to have a result more like a baked fish, it can be quickly browned in butter or oil before pressure cooking. (See the recipe for mackerel on page 33.)

Frozen fish is often more readily available than wet fish from the fishmonger and has the advantage of being portioned and ready to use. **It may be cooked from frozen**, giving the same timings for fillets and one minute longer for steaks, cutlets or whole fish.

After cooking, fish can be rather delicate to handle, therefore the following points can assist. If the fish is to be cooked on the trivet, always grease this first to prevent sticking. Alternatively, the fish can be placed on a piece of greased greaseproof paper which can then be used to lift the fish easily out of the cooker. Some pressure cookers have a wide, shallow separator; this is very useful as it can be used as the cooking container, again lightly greased.

The cooking liquor will be well-flavoured and can be used as the basis for a sauce to be served with the fish.

General instructions for cooking fish

1. Choose fish that looks and smells absolutely fresh – firm flesh, moist shiny scales and bright eyes. If possible cook on the day of purchase as fish does not keep well.
2. Clean, trim, scale and wash the fish according to its kind. Dry and season lightly.
3. A minimum of 300 ml/$\frac{1}{2}$ pint of liquid should be used for cooking. This can be water, milk, fish stock, wine or a Court bouillon, see recipe right.
4. H pressure may be used for cooking all fish.
5. Use the trivet to raise the fish out of the cooking

liquid for steaming. Always grease lightly.

6. Time carefully, as most fish have delicate flesh which can be spoilt by overcooking.

7. Always reduce pressure immediately and quickly.

8. Make use of all or part of the cooking liquid to make a well-flavoured accompanying sauce, or garnish with lemon wedges, parsley or savoury butters.

Court bouillon

Peel and chop 1 small onion. Put into a saucepan with 1 bay leaf, a few parsley stalks, a strip of lemon peel, 150 ml/¼ pint water and 150 ml/¼ pint white wine. Season lightly with salt and pepper. Bring to the boil, cover with a lid and simmer, over a low heat, for 15 minutes. Cool slightly, strain then use as desired.

Timetable for cooking fish

WHITE FISH	H (15 lb) PRESSURE	L (7½ lb) PRESSURE
Cod, Haddock, Hake:		
fillets	3 minutes	4 minutes
2.5 cm/1 inch steaks, cutlets	4 minutes	6 minutes
whole pieces	5–6 minutes per 500 g/1 lb	7–8 minutes per 500 g/1 lb
Plaice and Sole:		
fillets	3 minutes	4 minutes
whole small fish	5 minutes	8 minutes
Turbot and Halibut:		
fillets	3 minutes	4 minutes
2.5 cm/1 inch steaks	4 minutes	6 minutes
whole pieces	5–6 minutes per 500 g/1 lb	7–8 minutes per 500 g/1 lb
Bream:		
fillets	3 minutes	4 minutes
small whole fish	4–5 minutes	6–8 minutes

Skate:		
wings	4–5 minutes	6–8 minutes
		(depending on thickness)
Whiting:		
whole fish	5–6 minutes	7–8 minutes
		(depending on size)
OILY FISH	H (15 lb) PRESSURE	L (7½ lb) PRESSURE
Herring and Mackerel:		
fillets	4 minutes	6 minutes
whole fish	5–7 minutes	7–9 minutes
		(depending on size)
Red and Grey Mullet:	5–7 minutes	7–9 minutes
		(depending on size)
Trout:		
whole fish	5–6 minutes	7–8 minutes
		(depending on size)
Salmon and Trout:		
2.5 cm/1 inch steaks	4–6 minutes	6–8 minutes
small whole or pieces	6 minutes per 500 g/1 lb	9 minutes per 500 g/1 lb

Basic white sauce

If you are making this sauce in the cooker, and have already cooked your fish, remember to rinse and dry the cooker before use. This quantity of sauce will serve four.

METRIC	IMPERIAL
25 g butter or margarine	1 oz butter or margarine
25 g flour	1 oz flour
300 ml cooking liquid	½ pint cooking liquid
150 ml milk	¼ pint milk
salt	salt
freshly ground black pepper	freshly ground black pepper

METHOD

Melt the butter or margarine in the cooker. Stir in the flour and cook for 1 minute, stirring constantly. Remove from the heat and gradually add the cooking liquid and milk. Return the cooker to the heat and bring to the boil, stirring constantly. Simmer for 1 or 2 minutes before adding salt, pepper and one of the following suggested flavourings.

Variations:

Prawn or shrimp sauce

Add 50 g/2 oz cooked shelled prawns or shrimps to the Basic white sauce. A little anchovy essence may be added for a pale pink colour. Serve with any white fish.

Anchovy sauce

Add 2 × 5 ml spoons/2 teaspoons anchovy essence and 1 × 5 ml spoon/1 teaspoon lemon juice to the Basic white sauce. Serve with any white fish, and may also be served with herrings or mackerel.

Parsley sauce

Add 2 × 15 ml spoons/2 tablespoons freshly chopped parsley to the Basic white sauce. Serve with any white fish.

Egg sauce

Add 2 chopped, hard-boiled eggs with 1 × 5 ml spoon/1 teaspoon finely chopped fresh chives or parsley to the Basic white sauce. Serve with any white fish.

Mornay sauce

Add 75 g/3 oz grated cheese to the Basic white sauce. Sprinkle a further 25 g/1 oz of grated cheese over the completed dish and brown under a hot grill. Serve with any white fish.

Mustard sauce

Add 1 × 5 ml spoon/1 teaspoon dry English mustard, 2 × 5 ml spoons/2 teaspoons lemon juice or wine vinegar and 1 × 5 ml spoon/1 teaspoon sugar to the Basic white sauce. Serve with herrings or mackerel.

Cider sauce

Use 300 ml/½ pint cider instead of the cooking liquid. Make as for Basic white sauce. Serve with any oily fish.

Savoury butters

These make a delicious addition to any fish. If you own a home freezer they can be made and stored in handy amounts. To serve from the freezer cut into slices, using a knife dipped in hot water.

Maître d'hôtel butter

METRIC	IMPERIAL
100 g butter, softened	4 oz butter, softened
1 × 15 ml spoon freshly chopped parsley	1 tablespoon freshly chopped parsley
1 × 5 ml spoon lemon juice	1 teaspoon lemon juice
salt	salt
freshly ground black pepper	freshly ground black pepper

METHOD

Blend the ingredients to a soft paste, adding salt and pepper to taste. Form a roll that can be sliced or shape into small pats. Wrap in greaseproof paper or foil and chill in the refrigerator until very firm.

Variations:

Chive butter

Make as for Maître d'hôtel butter but substitute 2 × 15 ml spoons/2 tablespoons finely chopped chives for the parsley.

Lemon butter

Make as for Maître d'hôtel butter but substitute 2 × 5 ml spoons/2 teaspoons finely grated lemon rind for the parsley.

Savoury seafood starters

This recipe can be varied by substituting the prawns with cooked flaked smoked haddock, canned pink salmon or tuna fish.

METRIC	IMPERIAL
a little butter or margarine for greasing	a little butter or margarine for greasing
100 g shelled prawns	4 oz shelled prawns
1 large egg	1 large egg
4 × 15 ml spoons double cream	4 tablespoons double cream
4 × 15 ml spoons milk	4 tablespoons milk
25 g finely grated Cheddar cheese	1 oz finely grated Cheddar cheese
salt	salt
freshly ground black pepper	freshly ground black pepper
300 ml water	½ pint water
To finish:	**To finish:**
4 × 15 ml spoons fresh white breadcrumbs	4 tablespoons fresh white breadcrumbs
25 g finely grated Cheddar cheese	1 oz finely grated Cheddar cheese
1 × 5 ml spoon finely chopped fresh parsley	1 teaspoon finely chopped fresh parsley

H Pressure – 3 minutes

METHOD

Lightly grease 4 ovenproof ramekin dishes with a little butter or margarine. Divide the prawns equally between the dishes. Beat together the egg, cream, milk, cheese and a little salt and pepper and pour over the prawns. Put the water into the cooker with the trivet, rim side down. Stand the dishes on the trivet and cover each with a piece of greased greaseproof paper or aluminium foil. Close the cooker, bring to H pressure and cook for 3 minutes. Reduce pressure slowly.

While the prawns are cooking, mix together the breadcrumbs, cheese and parsley. Lift the hot dishes out of the cooker, remove the paper or foil and add a little breadcrumb topping to each dish. Place under a preheated hot grill until golden brown. Serve hot. Garnish each dish with an unshelled prawn, if liked.

Mackerel with lemon and chives

METRIC	IMPERIAL
75 g fresh white breadcrumbs	3 oz fresh white breadcrumbs
finely grated rind of 1 lemon	finely grated rind of 1 lemon
juice of 1 lemon	juice of 1 lemon
1 × 15 ml spoon finely chopped chives	1 tablespoon finely chopped chives
salt	salt
freshly ground black pepper	freshly ground black pepper
1 egg, beaten	1 egg, beaten
4 mackerel, cleaned and heads removed	4 mackerel, cleaned and heads removed
25 g butter	1 oz butter
2 × 15 ml spoons cooking oil	2 tablespoons cooking oil
300 ml water	½ pint water
a little butter or margarine for greasing	a little butter or margarine for greasing
lemon wedges to finish	lemon wedges to finish

H Pressure – 5 minutes

METHOD

Mix together the breadcrumbs, lemon rind and juice and chives with salt and pepper. Bind the mixture with the beaten egg. Divide the stuffing between the fish and press well into the cavity, secure the opening with a wooden cocktail stick. Heat the butter and oil in the cooker and quickly brown the fish on both sides, lift out and drain off the butter and oil. Put the water into the cooker. Grease the trivet with a little butter or margarine and place into the cooker. Lay the fish, head to tail on the trivet. Close the cooker, bring to H pressure and cook for 5 minutes. Reduce the pressure quickly and remove the cocktail sticks. Garnish the mackerel with chopped chives and parsley sprigs, if liked, and serve with wedges of lemon.

Cider soused mackerel; Trout maître d'hôtel;
Stuffed plaice with wine sauce

Cider soused mackerel

METRIC	IMPERIAL
4 medium mackerel, filleted	4 medium mackerel, filleted
300 ml dry cider	½ pint dry cider
1 onion, peeled and thinly sliced	1 onion, peeled and thinly sliced
8 black peppercorns	8 black peppercorns
1 bay leaf	1 bay leaf
a little salt	a little salt

H Pressure – 5 minutes

METHOD

Roll the fish up from head end to tail end and secure with cocktail sticks, if necessary. Put the cider into the cooker, with the sliced onion. Add the mackerel, peppercorns, bay leaf and a little salt. Close the cooker, bring to H pressure and cook for 5 minutes. Reduce the pressure quickly. Carefully lift out the fish, transfer to a serving dish and remove the cocktail sticks, if used. Pour over the cooking liquid and onion, remove the bay leaf. Cool thoroughly before serving.

Trout maître d'hôtel

METRIC	IMPERIAL
100 g butter, softened	4 oz butter, softened
1 × 15 ml spoon freshly chopped parsley	1 tablespoon freshly chopped parsley
1 × 5 ml spoon lemon juice	1 teaspoon lemon juice
salt	salt
freshly ground black pepper	freshly ground black pepper
4 trout, cleaned and fins removed	4 trout, cleaned and fins removed
300 ml water	½ pint water
a little butter or margarine for greasing	a little butter or margarine for greasing

H Pressure – 4 minutes

METHOD

Mix together the butter, parsley and lemon juice with a little salt and pepper. Chill half the butter, divide the remainder into 4 and spread inside the cavity of each fish. Put the water into the cooker. Grease the trivet with a little butter or margarine and place in the cooker. Lay the fish, head to tail on the trivet. Close the cooker, bring to H pressure and cook for 4 minutes. Reduce the pressure quickly. Lift out the fish and top each with a piece of chilled butter.

Stuffed plaice with wine sauce

H Pressure – 4 minutes

METRIC
25 g butter or margarine
1 small onion, peeled and
  chopped
4 rashers unsmoked streaky
  bacon, rinded and finely
  chopped
50 g mushrooms, cleaned and
  finely chopped
100 g fresh white breadcrumbs
1 × 2.5 ml spoon dried thyme
salt
freshly ground black pepper
1 egg, beaten
8 fillets of plaice, skinned
1 bay leaf
300 ml milk
a little butter or margarine
  for greasing
Sauce:
25 g butter or margarine
25 g flour
150 ml dry white wine

IMPERIAL
1 oz butter or margarine
1 small onion, peeled and
  chopped
4 rashers unsmoked streaky
  bacon, rinded and finely
  chopped
2 oz mushrooms, cleaned
  and finely chopped
4 oz fresh white breadcrumbs
½ teaspoon dried thyme
salt
freshly ground black pepper
1 egg, beaten
8 fillets of plaice, skinned
1 bay leaf
½ pint milk
a little butter or margarine
  for greasing
Sauce:
1 oz butter or margarine
1 oz flour
¼ pint dry white wine

METHOD
Heat the butter or margarine in the cooker. Fry the onion, bacon and mushrooms until they begin to colour, lift out and drain well. Add the bacon mixture to the breadcrumbs, thyme, salt and pepper and bind with the egg. Divide the stuffing between the fillets, placing the stuffing on the skinned side and spreading over evenly. Roll the fish up from the tail end and secure with cocktail sticks, if necessary.

Put the bay leaf and milk into the cooker. Grease the trivet with a little butter or margarine and place into the cooker. Place the fillets, standing up on end onto the trivet. Stand them close together to support each other. Close the cooker, bring to H pressure and cook for 4 minutes. Reduce the pressure quickly. Lift out the fish, remove the cocktail sticks if used, and keep hot.

Strain off the milk and reserve, discard the bay leaf. Rinse and dry the cooker. Melt the butter or margarine in the cooker, add the flour and cook for a few moments. Remove from the heat and stir in the reserved milk then add the wine. Return to the heat and bring to the boil, stirring continuously. Simmer for 1 minute. Taste and adjust the seasoning as necessary before pouring around the fish.

Plaice with mushroom sauce

METRIC	IMPERIAL
300 ml milk	½ pint milk
100 g mushrooms, cleaned and thinly sliced	4 oz mushrooms, cleaned and thinly sliced
1 small onion, chopped	1 small onion, chopped
1 bay leaf	1 bay leaf
a little butter or margarine for greasing	a little butter or margarine for greasing
4 fillets of plaice, skinned	4 fillets of plaice, skinned
salt	salt
freshly ground black pepper	freshly ground black pepper
25 g butter	1 oz butter
Sauce:	**Sauce:**
25 g butter	1 oz butter
25 g flour	1 oz flour
approx. 150 ml milk	approx. ¼ pint milk

H Pressure – 3 minutes

METHOD

Put the milk, mushrooms, onion and bay leaf into the cooker. Lightly grease the trivet with a little butter or margarine and place into the cooker. Season the fillets with salt and pepper and fold over. Stand on the trivet, each fillet topped with a knob of the butter. Close the cooker, bring to H pressure and cook for 3 minutes. Reduce the pressure quickly. Lift out the fish and keep hot.

Strain the milk into a measuring jug, discard the bay leaf. Return the onion and mushrooms to the cooker. Make up the milk to 450 ml/¾ pint with the milk for the sauce. Melt the butter in the cooker, stir in the flour and cook for 1 minute. Remove from the heat and gradually stir in the flavoured milk. Return to the heat and bring to the boil, stirring constantly. Simmer for 1 minute, taste and adjust the seasoning as necessary before pouring over the fish. Garnish with a lemon twist and parsley sprigs, if liked.

Below: Plaice with mushroom sauce; Right: Halibut with prawn sauce; Haddock mornay

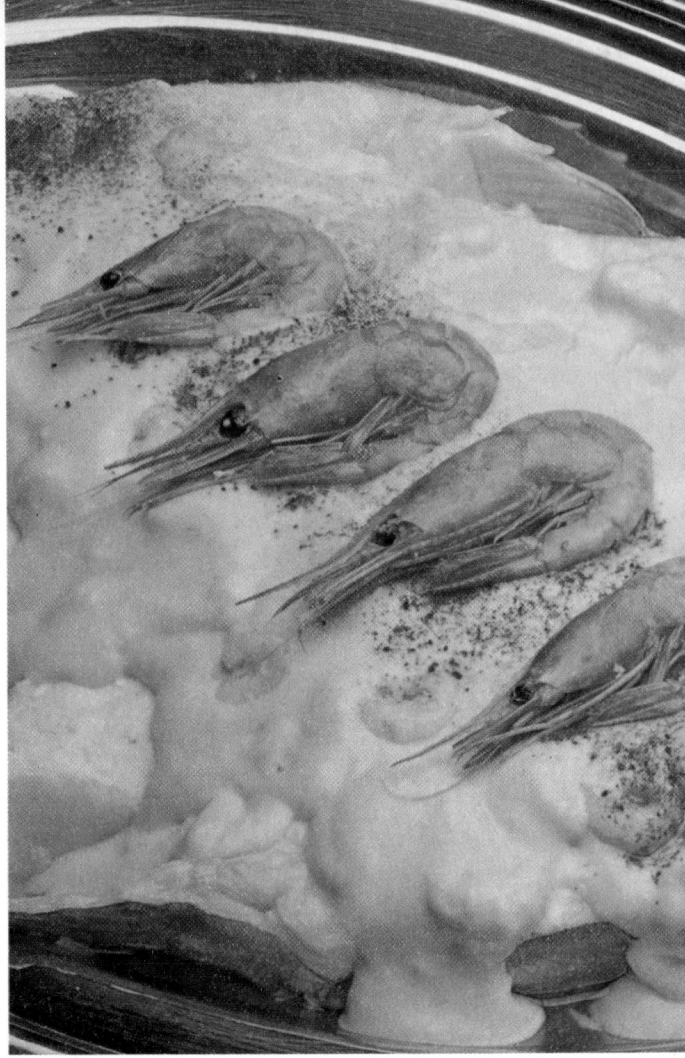

Halibut with prawn sauce

METRIC	IMPERIAL
1 bay leaf	1 bay leaf
a few sprigs of parsley	a few sprigs of parsley
a few black peppercorns	a few black peppercorns
300 ml milk	½ pint milk
a little butter or margarine for greasing	a little butter or margarine for greasing
4 halibut steaks	4 halibut steaks
salt	salt
freshly ground black pepper	freshly ground black pepper
Sauce:	**Sauce:**
25 g butter or margarine	1 oz butter or margarine
25 g flour	1 oz flour
approx. 150 ml milk	approx. ¼ pint milk
75 g shelled prawns	3 oz shelled prawns
1–2 × 5 ml spoons anchovy essence	1–2 teaspoons anchovy essence
a little paprika pepper	a little paprika pepper

H Pressure – 4 minutes

METHOD

Put the bay leaf, parsley, peppercorns and milk into the cooker. Grease the trivet with a little butter or margarine and place into the cooker. Place the fish on top of the trivet and sprinkle with a little salt and pepper. Close the cooker, bring to H pressure and cook for 4 minutes. Reduce the

pressure quickly. Lift out the fish, transfer to a warmed serving dish and keep hot.

Strain the milk and discard the herbs and peppercorns. Make the milk up to 450 ml/¾ pint with the milk for the sauce. Rinse and dry the cooker. Melt the butter or margarine in the cooker, add the flour and cook for a few moments. Remove from the heat and add the milk, stirring well. Return to the heat and bring to the boil, stirring continuously. Add the prawns, reserving a few for garnish, and add sufficient anchovy essence to give a pale pink colour. Simmer for 1 minute, taste and adjust the seasoning as necessary before pouring over the halibut. Garnish with a few prawns and a light sprinkling of paprika pepper.

Haddock mornay

Other white fish can be substituted for the haddock in this recipe. Refer to the cooking chart on page 31 for each cooking time.

METRIC	IMPERIAL
1 bay leaf	1 bay leaf
a few sprigs of parsley	a few sprigs of parsley
a few black peppercorns	a few black peppercorns
300 ml milk	½ pint milk
a little butter or margarine for greasing	a little butter or margarine for greasing
750 g haddock fillets, cut	1½ lb haddock fillets, cut
into 4 pieces	into 4 pieces
salt	salt
freshly ground black pepper	freshly ground black pepper
Sauce:	**Sauce:**
25 g butter or margarine	1 oz butter or margarine
25 g flour	1 oz flour
approx. 150 ml milk	approx. ¼ pint milk
100 g cheese, grated	4 oz cheese, grated

H Pressure – 4 minutes

METHOD

Put the bay leaf, parsley, peppercorns and milk into the cooker. Grease the trivet with a little butter or margarine and place in the cooker. Place the pieces of haddock on the trivet and sprinkle with a little salt and pepper. Close the cooker, bring to H pressure and cook for 4 minutes. Reduce the pressure quickly. Lift out the fish and transfer to a lightly greased flameproof dish. Keep warm.

Strain the milk, discarding the herbs and peppercorns. Make the milk up to 450 ml/¾ pint with the milk for the sauce. Rinse and dry the cooker. Melt the butter or margarine in the cooker. Add the flour and cook for a few moments. Remove from the heat and add the milk, stirring well. Return to the heat and bring to the boil, stirring continuously, simmer for 1 minute. Remove from the heat and stir in 75 g/3 oz of the cheese with extra salt, if necessary. Pour the sauce over the fish, sprinkle with the remaining cheese and brown under a hot grill.

Smoked haddock mousse

METRIC

600 ml water
a little butter or margarine
  for greasing
350 g smoked haddock fillets
25 g butter or margarine
25 g flour
150 ml milk
50 g mushrooms, cleaned and
  finely chopped
1 × 2.5 ml spoon dried
  marjoram
2 eggs, beaten
2 × 15 ml spoons single
  cream
salt
freshly ground black pepper
a little lemon juice

To finish:

1 egg, hard boiled
few sprigs of fresh parsley

IMPERIAL

1 pint water
a little butter or margarine
  for greasing
12 oz smoked haddock fillets
1 oz butter or margarine
1 oz flour
¼ pint milk
2 oz mushrooms, cleaned and
  finely chopped
½ teaspoon dried marjoram
2 eggs, beaten
2 tablespoons single cream
salt
freshly ground black pepper
a little lemon juice

To finish:

1 egg, hard boiled
few sprigs of fresh parsley

H Pressure – 5 minutes to cook fish
H Pressure – 5 minutes to cook mousse

METHOD

Put 300 ml/½ pint water into the cooker. Grease the trivet with a little butter or margarine. Place trivet in the cooker and lay the fish on top. Close the cooker, bring to H pressure and cook for 5 minutes. Reduce the pressure quickly. Lift out the fish carefully remove any skin and flake the flesh with a fork.

Melt the butter or margarine in a saucepan, add the flour and cook for a few moments. Remove from the heat and stir in the milk. Return to the heat, bring to the boil, stirring continuously and cook for 1 minute. Stir this sauce into the fish with the mushrooms, marjoram, eggs, cream, salt and pepper. Transfer to a lightly greased 600 ml/1 pint oven-proof dish; cover with a piece of greaseproof paper. Put the remaining water and the trivet into the cooker, adding a little lemon juice. Stand the covered dish on the trivet, close the cooker, bring to H pressure and cook for 5 minutes. Reduce the pressure quickly. Lift out the mousse, remove the paper and cool thoroughly.

To serve, turn out on to a serving dish and garnish with sliced hard-boiled egg and parsley.

Devonshire herrings

METRIC	IMPERIAL
4 large herrings, filleted	4 large herrings, filleted
salt	salt
freshly ground black pepper	freshly ground black pepper
50 g fresh white breadcrumbs	2 oz fresh white breadcrumbs
1 × 5 ml spoon dried thyme	1 teaspoon dried thyme
1 dessert apple, peeled and	1 dessert apple, peeled and
finely chopped	finely chopped
1 small onion, grated	1 small onion, grated
40 g butter or margarine	1½ oz butter or margarine
300 ml dry cider	½ pint dry cider
a little butter or margarine	a little butter or margarine
for greasing	for greasing
2 × 5 ml spoons cornflour	2 teaspoons cornflour

H Pressure – 6 minutes

METHOD

Place the filleted herrings on a board, skin side down and sprinkle with a little salt and pepper. Mix together the bread-crumbs, thyme, apple and onion. Bind with the melted butter or margarine. Divide the stuffing between the fillets and fold each fillet in half, secure with cocktail sticks if necessary. Put the cider into the cooker. Lightly grease the trivet with a little butter or margarine and place in the cooker. Stand the fish on the trivet. Close the cooker, bring to H pressure and cook for 6 minutes. Reduce the pressure quickly. Lift out the fish, remove the cocktail sticks if used, garnish with apple slices, and keep hot. Remove the trivet from the cooker. Return the open cooker to the heat and add the cornflour, blended with a little cold water. Bring to the boil, stirring constantly and simmer for 1 minute. Taste and adjust seasoning and pour over the fish.

Smoked haddock mousse;
Devonshire herrings

Piquant fish casserole

METRIC	IMPERIAL
50 g butter or margarine	2 oz butter or margarine
1 onion, peeled and chopped	1 onion, peeled and chopped
100 g button mushrooms, cleaned	4 oz button mushrooms, cleaned
750 g cod or haddock fillet, cut into 2.5 cm pieces	1½ lb cod or haddock fillet, cut into 1 inch pieces
1 × 415 g can lobster bisque soup	1 × 14½ oz can lobster bisque soup
a little water	a little water
1 × 15 ml spoon Worcestershire sauce	1 tablespoon Worcestershire sauce
1 bay leaf	1 bay leaf
salt	salt
freshly ground black pepper	freshly ground black pepper
2 × 5 ml spoons cornflour blended with a little cold water (optional)	2 teaspoons cornflour blended with a little cold water (optional)
a little freshly chopped parsley to finish	a little freshly chopped parsley to finish

H Pressure – 4 minutes

METHOD
Heat the butter or margarine in the cooker and lightly fry the onions and mushrooms, without colouring. Lift out and drain well. Add the fish and brown lightly, lift out and drain off excess butter or margarine. Add the can of soup and a quarter of a can of water with the Worcestershire sauce, bay leaf, salt and pepper and stir well. Return the fish and vegetables to the cooker. Close the cooker, bring to H pressure and cook for 4 minutes. Reduce the pressure quickly and remove the bay leaf. If liked, thicken the sauce with the blended cornflour. Stir into the liquid, bring to the boil, stirring constantly, and simmer for 1 minute. Taste and adjust the seasoning as necessary. Garnish with the chopped parsley.

Cod with orange topping

METRIC	IMPERIAL
75 g fresh white breadcrumbs	3 oz fresh white breadcrumbs
finely grated rind of 1 orange	finely grated rind of 1 orange
1 orange, peel and pith removed and chopped	1 orange, peel and pith removed and chopped
salt	salt
freshly ground black pepper	freshly ground black pepper
1 × 5 ml spoon dried marjoram	1 teaspoon dried marjoram
1 egg, beaten	1 egg, beaten
4 cod steaks or cutlets	4 cod steaks or cutlets
300 ml water	½ pint water
a little butter or margarine for greasing	a little butter or margarine for greasing
To finish:	**To finish:**
1 orange, sliced	1 orange, sliced
a few sprigs of parsley	a few sprigs of parsley

H Pressure – 4 minutes

METHOD
Mix together the breadcrumbs, orange rind, chopped orange, salt, pepper and marjoram with the egg. Divide between the 4 pieces of fish and spread to the edges of each. Put the water into the cooker. Grease the trivet with a little butter or margarine and place in the cooker. Carefully place the pieces of fish on top. Close the cooker, bring to H pressure and cook for 4 minutes. Reduce the pressure quickly. Carefully remove the cod from the cooker and serve with orange slices and sprigs of parsley.

Cod with orange topping; Seafood pilau; Piquant fish casserole

Seafood pilau

METRIC

2 × 15 ml spoons cooking oil
1 onion, peeled and chopped
1 green pepper, cored, seeded and chopped
50 g mushrooms, cleaned and sliced
600 ml white stock or water and ½ chicken stock cube
225 g long-grain rice
1 × 215 g can tuna fish, drained and flaked
100 g shelled prawns
1 × 5 ml spoon Worcestershire sauce

IMPERIAL

2 tablespoons cooking oil
1 onion, peeled and chopped
1 green pepper, cored, seeded and chopped
2 oz mushrooms, cleaned and sliced
1 pint white stock or water and ½ chicken stock cube
8 oz long-grain rice
1 × 7½ oz can tuna fish, drained and flaked
4 oz shelled prawns
1 teaspoon Worcestershire sauce

1 × 2.5 ml spoon dried thyme
salt
freshly ground black pepper
a little freshly chopped parsley for garnish

½ teaspoon dried thyme
salt
freshly ground black pepper
a little freshly chopped parsley for garnish

H Pressure – 6 minutes

METHOD

Heat the oil in the cooker, lightly fry the onion, pepper and mushrooms. Lift out and drain off any excess oil. Add the stock or water and stock cube, cooked vegetables and remaining ingredients, except the parsley, to the cooker, stir well. Close the cooker, bring to H pressure and cook for 6 minutes. Reduce the pressure quickly. Return the open cooker to a low heat and stir with a fork to separate the rice grains. Serve garnished with the chopped parsley, if liked.

Vegetables

Accurate timing for some pressure cooked foods is not as vital as it is for others; a few minutes longer for a beef casserole will not be a disaster. When cooking vegetables this is not the case, and careful timing is important for good results.

Many foods, vegetables in particular, quickly lose their nutritive value, colour and texture, if cooked incorrectly or for too long. This applies to any method of vegetable cooking, not just the pressure cooker.

However, vegetables cooked in a pressure cooker have several advantages: they are not immersed in water, therefore vitamin, mineral and colour loss is kept to a minimum; they are cooked in the absence of air, again aiding retention of nutrients; they are cooked quickly and a selection can be cooked together, without any fear of flavours intermingling, therefore saving fuel and washing-up.

Choice

Be selective when choosing vegetables. Tired and limp vegetables may be cheaper, but they will already have lost some of their nutritional value, colour and texture and nothing is able to reverse that.

With the modern techniques of transportation and storage, even the more exotic vegetables from abroad can be enjoyed in peak condition.

Preparation

Preparing vegetables for pressure cooking is just the same as for any other method of cooking. Outer skins are either scrubbed or peeled, damaged leaves discarded and the vegetables washed as near to the cooking time as possible. Vegetables should not be left

soaking for long periods, nor should green vegetables be shredded or chopped a long time before cooking as both these can lead to loss of nutrients.

Seasoning

Usually far less seasoning, particularly salt, is required for cooking vegetables in a pressure cooker. Salt is not dissolved in the cooking water but is sprinkled straight on to the vegetable. Therefore, to ensure an even distribution it is better to sprinkle salt over from a salt pot.

Cooking green vegetables

Green vegetables should *always* be put into the cooker after the water has been brought to the boil, just as you would do when cooking in a saucepan. This method ensures that pressure is reached quickly and prevents discoloration or overcooking.

Cooking a selection of vegetables

It is usual for more than one vegetable to be served for a meal. Therefore, if two or more vegetables can be cooked in the pressure cooker, the savings in both time and fuel become greater. However, to do this successfully root vegetables, such as potatoes or carrots, must be cut up a little smaller so they will cook in the 4 minutes required for most green vegetables. Determining how small these pieces have to be can be difficult until you have practised a few times. This may cause so much frustration, that vegetable cooking in the pressure cooker is sometimes assumed to be a failure. Potatoes are probably the most difficult to gauge but the following guide gives an indication to their size for cooking in 4 minutes at HIGH pressure.

small new potatoes approximately 25 to 40 g/1 to 1$\frac{1}{2}$ oz, leave whole

old or new potatoes approximately 50 g/2 oz, cut in half

old or new potatoes approximately 75 g/3 oz, cut into three even-sized pieces

old or new potatoes approximately 100 g/4 oz, cut into quarters

continue in this way for larger potatoes.

Timetable for fresh vegetables

VEGETABLE	PREPARATION	H (15 lb) PRESSURE	L (7½ lb) PRESSURE
Artichoke – Globe	Remove outside damaged leaves and stalk. Trim points from leaves. Wash well. Cook on trivet	Small: 6 minutes Large: 10–12 minutes	10 minutes 15 minutes
Jerusalem	Scrub well. Cook on trivet.	4–5 minutes	6–7 minutes
Asparagus	Cut off hard ends. Tie into bundles of 4–6 spears. Lay on trivet.	Young: 2 minutes Older: 4 minutes	4 minutes 6 minutes
Beans – Broad	Remove from pods. Cook in separator.	4 minutes	6 minutes
French	Top and tail. Wash. Cook in separator.	4 minutes	6 minutes
Runner	Top and tail. Wash and slice, string older beans. Cook in separator.	4 minutes	6 minutes
Beetroot	Trim off all but 2.5 cm/1 inch of stalk and root. Wash carefully without breaking skin. Cook without trivet. Peel when cooked.	Small: 10 minutes 600 ml/1 pint water Medium: 15–20 minutes 900 ml/1½ pints water Large: 25–30 minutes 1.2 litres/2 pints water	15 minutes 20–30 minutes
Broccoli	Cut off stalk ends. Wash well. Cook in separator.	3–4 minutes	5–6 minutes
Brussels sprouts	Discard damaged leaves, trim and cut a cross into stalk. Cook in separator.	Button: 3 minutes Medium: 4 minutes	5 minutes 6 minutes
Cabbage – Green, white, spring green	Discard damaged leaves. Remove stalks, shred or chop. Cook in separator.	4 minutes	5 minutes
Red	Cook on its own as above.	4 minutes	5 minutes
Carrots	Top and tail and scrape. Wash. Cook on trivet or in separator.	Young: whole, 4 minutes Old: sliced or quartered 4 minutes	6 minutes 6 minutes
Cauliflower	Remove coarse stalks, leave whole or divide into florets. Wash. Cook on trivet or in separator.	Whole: 5–8 minutes Florets: 4 minutes	7–9 minutes 5 minutes
Celeriac	Peel, cut into 2.5 cm/1 inch cubes, wash. Cook in separator.	4 minutes	6 minutes
Celery	Cut off leaves and root. Cut into 5 cm/2 inch lengths. Scrub under running water. Cook on trivet or in separator.	4–6 minutes	7–9 minutes
Chicory	Trim away wilted or damaged leaves. Wash well. Cook on trivet with a little lemon juice and butter.	Small: 4 minutes Medium: 6 minutes	6 minutes 9 minutes

Basic method for cooking a selection of vegetables

1. Put 300 ml/½ pint water into the cooker with the trivet, rim side down.
2. Place piles of prepared root vegetables such as carrots, onions and potatoes on the trivet and season lightly with salt.
3. Put the open cooker on to a high heat and bring the water to the boil.
4. Place the prepared green vegetables such as beans, Brussels sprouts and shredded cabbage in the separators and season lightly with salt. Stand the separators on top of the root vegetables. At this stage the cooker must never be more than two-thirds full.
5. Close the cooker and, keeping the heat high, bring to H pressure, cook for 4 minutes. Reduce pressure immediately and quickly.

The vegetables will not require straining. They can be served with an appropriate sauce, butter or margarine and freshly ground black pepper. The small amount of cooking liquid will contain those nutrients which have been lost from the vegetables during the cooking and is ideal for use in gravies, stocks or sauces.

Dried vegetables

Dried vegetables normally require long soaking and cooking to make them tender, but in a pressure cooker both processes can be considerably reduced.

VEGETABLE	PREPARATION	H (15 lb) PRESSURE	L (7½ lb) PRESSURE
Corn on the Cob	Discard husks (leaves) and silks. Trim stalk. Cook on trivet or in separator.	Small: whole, 4 minutes Large: whole, 6 minutes	6 minutes 8 minutes
Courgettes	Top and tail, wash, slice 2.5 cm/1 inch thick. Cook in separator.	4 minutes	6 minutes
Fennel	Discard leaf tops. Wash. Cut into halves or quarters. Cook on trivet or in separator.	4–6 minutes	6–8 minutes
Leeks	Trim off tops and roots. Wash thoroughly. Cut into 5 cm/2 inch lengths. If large split lengthways first. Cook in separator.	4 minutes	6 minutes
Marrow	Peel. Cut into thick 2.5 cm/1 inch slices, remove seeds. Cook on trivet or in separator.	3–4 minutes	5–6 minutes
Onions	Peel. Cook whole on trivet, sliced in separator.	Small: whole or sliced, 4 minutes Large: whole, 6–8 minutes	6 minutes 8–10 minutes
Parsnips	Peel, cut into 2.5 cm/1 inch cubes. Cook on trivet or in separator.	4 minutes	6 minutes
For roasting:	Cut into halves. Complete cooking in a hot oven.	2 minutes	3 minutes
Peas	Shell. Cook in separator.	3–4 minutes	5–6 minutes
Peppers – Red and green	Remove core and seeds. Usually cooked stuffed on trivet.	4–5 minutes	6–7 minutes
Potatoes – New	Scrape or scrub. Cook on trivet or in separator. Leave whole or cut up as indicated on page 43.	4 minutes	6 minutes
Old	Peel. Cut up as indicated on page 43.	4 minutes	6 minutes
For roasting:	Cut into halves or quarters. Complete cooking in a hot oven.	2 minutes	3 minutes
Spinach	Wash thoroughly under cold running water. Discard coarse stalks and damaged leaves. Cook without trivet and only 2 × 15 ml spoons/2 tablespoons water.	To pressure only	1 minute
Swedes	Peel, cut into 2.5 cm/1 inch cubes. Cook on trivet or in separator.	4 minutes	6 minutes
Turnips	As for swedes unless very small when they can be cooked whole.	4 minutes	6 minutes

General instructions

1. Dried vegetables swell to at least double their original size and they also have a tendency to boil and froth during cooking. For these reasons, the pressure cooker should not be more than a third full when all the vegetables and liquid have been added. The trivet is not used.
2. Weigh the vegetables, put into a large basin and add sufficient boiling water to cover. Leave for 1 hour.
3. Strain off the liquid and make up to 1.2 litres/2 pints for each 500 g/1 lb of dried weight of vegetables.
4. Put the liquid and vegetables into the cooker with a little salt and pepper. Bring to the boil and skim well. Lower the heat to simmer. Close the cooker and, without altering the heat, bring to H pressure. Cook for the required time. Reduce pressure *slowly*.

Dried vegetables		
VEGETABLE	H (15 lb) PRESSURE	L (7½ lb) PRESSURE
Butter beans	20 minutes	35 minutes
Haricot beans – small	15 minutes	30 minutes
large	25 minutes	40 minutes
Lentils	15 minutes	30 minutes
Peas – split	15 minutes	30 minutes
whole	20 minutes	35 minutes
Soya beans	20 minutes	35 minutes

Timetable for blanching vegetables

VEGETABLE	PREPARATION	M (10 lb) PRESSURE	L (7½ lb) PRESSURE
Artichokes – Globe	Prepare as for cooking. Stand on trivet.	1 minute	2 minutes
Asparagus	Trim stalks, cut and sort into even-size thickness and length. Use separator.	To pressure only	1 minute
Beans – Broad	Shell and grade into sizes. Use separator.	Small: to pressure only Medium: 1 minute	1 minute 1½ minutes
French	Top and tail, leave whole. Use separator.	To pressure only	1 minute
Runner	String and slice thickly. Use separator.	To pressure only	1 minute
Beetroot – Small whole	Scald in boiling water, rub off skins. Use separator.	10–15 minutes	15–20 minutes
Sliced	Prepare as above and slice. Use separator.	6 minutes	9 minutes
Broccoli	Trim away woody stalks. Use separator.	1 minute	1½ minutes
Brussels sprouts	Choose small even-sized sprouts. Trim outside leaves. Use separator.	1 minute	1½ minutes
Cabbage – Red or white	Wash and shred. Use separator.	To pressure only	1 minute
Carrots – Young	Scrub and leave whole. Use separator.	2 minutes	3 minutes
Large	Scrape and slice. Use separator.	4 minutes	6 minutes
Cauliflower	Only freeze very firm compact cauliflower. Divide into florets no larger than 5 cm/2 inch across. Use separator.	1 minute	1½ minutes
Celery – Young hearts	Trim and scrub. Use trivet.	1 minute	1½ minutes
Stalks	Scrub, cut into 5 cm/2 inch lengths. Use separator.	2 minutes	3 minutes
Corn on the Cob	Use only young tender cobs. Remove husk and silks. Grade to size. On trivet or small in separator.	Small: 2 minutes Large: 3 minutes	3 minutes 4 minutes
Courgettes	Use young even-sized courgettes. Slice in half lengthways or slice 2.5 cm/1 inch thick. Use separator.	To pressure only	1 minute
Leeks	Discard damaged outer leaves. Wash well. Slice 2.5 cm/1 inch thick. Use separator.	1 minute	2 minutes
Marrow	Peel, remove seeds. Cut into large pieces. Use separator.	To pressure only	1 minute
Parsnips	Choose young parsnips. Peel, cut into 2.5 cm/1 inch cubes or pieces. Use separator.	1 minute	2 minutes
Peas	Choose young peas. Shell. Use separator.	To pressure only	1 minute
Spinach	Choose young fresh spinach. Wash very thoroughly. Use separator, blanch in small quantities.	To pressure only	30 seconds
Swedes	Peel and dice. Use separator.	1 minute	2 minutes
Turnips	Choose young small turnips, leave whole, peel. Dice older turnips. Use trivet or separator.	Small whole or diced: 2 minutes	3 minutes

Blanching vegetables for the home freezer

If you own a home freezer and can take advantage of seasonal vegetables at lower prices, or if you grow your own vegetables, the pressure cooker can be used very successfully for blanching, prior to freezing.

One manufacturer now offers a blanching basket for the pressure cooker but if you do not have one of these, the vegetables are piled on the trivet or into the separators.

The usual 300 ml/½ pint of water is all that is required. and the cooker is closed, therefore greatly reducing the amount of steam normally associated with blanching. The water must always be boiling before each batch of vegetables is added.

Choice and preparation

Vegetables for freezing must be in perfect condition otherwise the results will be disappointing. Preparation is just as for the saucepan method but with the advantage that generally, in the pressure cooker, slightly larger amounts can be blanched at one time. After blanching, the vegetables must be plunged immediately into iced water to prevent over processing. Therefore, if it can be planned, make large quantities of ice-cubes in advance. Once made, they can be stored in polythene bags in the freezer.

After cooking, drain the vegetables well before freezing.

Cooking frozen vegetables

As blanching partially cooks vegetables, they do not require as long a cooking time as their fresh counterpart.

It is not really worth cooking frozen vegetables on their own in the pressure cooker, but with a selection of other vegetables or to complete a dish it is advantageous. Always cook these vegetables from their frozen state, as the thawing time in the cooker makes up for the shorter cooking time they require.

Artichokes vinaigrette

Artichokes vinaigrette

METRIC	IMPERIAL
4 globe artichokes	*4 globe artichokes*
300 ml water	*½ pint water*
a little salt	*a little salt*
Vinaigrette dressing:	**Vinaigrette dressing:**
150 ml oil	*¼ pint oil*
3 × 15 ml spoons wine vinegar	*3 tablespoons wine vinegar*
1 garlic clove crushed with 1 × 2.5 ml spoon salt	*1 garlic clove crushed with ½ teaspoon salt*
freshly ground black pepper	*freshly ground black pepper*
1 × 15 ml spoon freshly chopped thyme or parsley	*1 tablespoon freshly chopped thyme or parsley*

H Pressure – 10 minutes

METHOD

Remove the stem of each artichoke and trim the base leaves so that they will stand upright. Lay the artichokes on their sides and slice 1 cm/½ inch off the top of the centre cone of leaves. Trim off the points of the rest of the leaves with scissors. Wash well under cold running water.

Put water and the trivet into the cooker and bring to the boil. Stand the artichokes upright on the trivet and sprinkle very lightly with salt. Close the cooker and bring to H pressure, cook for 10 minutes. Reduce the pressure quickly. Lift out the artichokes and cool. Put the oil and vinegar in a bowl and beat with a fork until thick. Beat in the garlic, black pepper and thyme or parsley. Serve the artichokes either with a little dressing spooned over them or plain, with the dressing in a side dish.

Onions provençale

An interesting hors d'oeuvre or vegetable. If liked, serve cold as an hors d'oeuvre, garnished with parsley.

METRIC	IMPERIAL
2 × 15 ml spoons olive or cooking oil	2 tablespoons olive or cooking oil
8 small onions, peeled	8 small onions, peeled
1 × 400 g can tomatoes, chopped	1 × 14 oz can tomatoes, chopped
150 ml dry white wine	¼ pint dry white wine
1 × 15 ml spoon freshly chopped parsley	1 tablespoon freshly chopped parsley
salt	salt
freshly ground black pepper	freshly ground black pepper
1 × 2.5 ml spoon sweet basil	½ teaspoon sweet basil

H Pressure – 6 minutes

METHOD
Heat the oil in the cooker and sauté the onions until just beginning to colour. Add all the remaining ingredients. Close the cooker, bring to H pressure and cook for 6 minutes. Reduce the pressure quickly.

Vegetable and nut pilaf

This pilaf makes an interesting accompaniment to fried chicken and grilled meats. It can also be served cold with cold meats.

METRIC	IMPERIAL
2 × 15 ml spoons cooking oil	2 tablespoons cooking oil
1 onion, peeled and coarsely chopped	1 onion, peeled and coarsely chopped
3 stalks celery, scrubbed and finely chopped	3 stalks celery, scrubbed and finely chopped
1 green pepper, cored, seeded and coarsely chopped	1 green pepper, cored, seeded and coarsely chopped
225 g long-grain patna rice	8 oz long-grain patna rice
600 ml hot poultry stock or water and ½ chicken stock cube	1 pint hot poultry stock or water and ½ chicken stock cube
salt	salt
freshly ground black pepper	freshly ground black pepper
25 g shelled walnuts, coarsely chopped	1 oz shelled walnuts, coarsely chopped
50 g roasted unsalted peanuts	2 oz roasted unsalted peanuts

H Pressure – 5 minutes

METHOD
Heat the oil in the cooker, sauté the vegetables for a few moments without colouring. Add the rice and cook until all the oil is absorbed. Add the stock or water and stock cube, salt and pepper and stir well. Close the cooker, bring to H pressure and cook for 5 minutes. Reduce the pressure quickly. Return the open cooker to the heat, add the nuts and stir with a fork to separate the rice grains.

Stuffed marrow rings

METRIC	IMPERIAL
25 g lard	1 oz lard
1 small onion, peeled and finely chopped	1 small onion, peeled and finely chopped
500 g sausagemeat	1 lb sausagemeat
1 hard-boiled egg, chopped	1 hard-boiled egg, chopped
large pinch mixed herbs	large pinch mixed herbs
salt	salt
freshly ground black pepper	freshly ground black pepper
1 marrow, peeled	1 marrow, peeled
450 ml hot brown stock or water and ½ beef stock cube	¾ pint hot brown stock or water and ½ beef stock cube
2 × 5 ml spoons cornflour	2 teaspoons cornflour
little cold water	little cold water

H Pressure – 5 minutes

METHOD
Heat the lard in the cooker and gently fry the onion and sausagemeat until both are just beginning to colour. Lift out and drain well. Drain off excess lard from the cooker. Add the egg, herbs, salt and pepper to the sausagemeat and onion and mix well. Cut the marrow into 5 cm/2 inch thick rings. Use a vegetable peeler or grapefruit knife to remove the seeds carefully without breaking the flesh. Fill each cavity with the meat filling, packing it well down. Put the stock or water and stock cube into the cooker with the trivet. Stand the filled marrow rings on the trivet. Close the cooker, bring to H pressure and cook for 5 minutes. Reduce the pressure quickly. Lift out the marrow to a warmed dish and keep hot. Remove the trivet and return the open cooker to the heat. Add the cornflour blended with a little cold water. Bring to the boil, stirring constantly. Taste and adjust the seasoning as necessary and serve the sauce poured around the marrow rings.

Braised celery with ham

METRIC
25 g butter
1 head of celery, scrubbed and
  cut into 5 cm pieces
2 carrots, peeled and sliced
300 ml hot brown stock or
  water and $\frac{1}{2}$ beef stock cube
100 g cooked shoulder of
  ham, cut into 2.5 cm strips
salt
freshly ground black pepper

IMPERIAL
1 oz butter
1 head of celery, scrubbed
  and cut into 2 inch pieces
2 carrots, peeled and sliced
$\frac{1}{2}$ pint hot brown stock or
  water and $\frac{1}{2}$ beef stock cube
4 oz cooked shoulder of ham,
  cut into 1 inch strips
salt
freshly ground black pepper

H Pressure – 5 minutes

METHOD
Heat the butter in the cooker. Sauté the celery and carrots
until both are beginning to colour. Remove the cooker from
the heat, stir in the stock or water and stock cube with the
ham and a little salt and pepper. Close the cooker, bring to
H pressure and cook for 5 minutes. Reduce the pressure
quickly.

Serve with pork or poultry.

*Vegetable and nut pilaf;
Onions provençale; Braised
celery with ham; Stuffed
marrow rings*

Stuffed peppers

METRIC	IMPERIAL
65 g long-grain rice	2½ oz long-grain rice
salt	salt
4 green peppers	4 green peppers
100 g cooked ham or streaky bacon, chopped	4 oz cooked ham or streaky bacon, chopped
100 g Cheddar cheese, grated	4 oz Cheddar cheese, grated
2 × 5 ml spoons Worcestershire sauce	2 teaspoons Worcestershire sauce
freshly ground black pepper	freshly ground black pepper
300 ml water	½ pint water

H Pressure – 5 minutes

METHOD

Cook the rice in plenty of boiling salted water until tender, about 12 to 15 minutes. Drain in a sieve and rinse with hot water. Carefully cut a hole around the stalk end of each pepper and remove the core and seeds. If necessary, cut a thin slice from the base of the pepper so that it will stand upright. Mix together the cooked rice, ham or bacon, cheese, Worcestershire sauce and a little salt and pepper. Pack the stuffing into each pepper, pressing it down well. Put the water and the trivet into the cooker. Stand the peppers upright on the trivet. Close the cooker, bring to H pressure and cook for 5 minutes. Reduce the pressure quickly.

Stuffed peppers

Scalloped potatoes and mushrooms

This dish is a good accompaniment to grilled meats.

METRIC	IMPERIAL
a little butter or margarine for greasing	a little butter or margarine for greasing
750 g potatoes, peeled and thinly sliced	1½ lb potatoes, peeled and thinly sliced
100 g mushrooms, cleaned and thinly sliced	4 oz mushrooms, cleaned and thinly sliced
1 small onion, peeled and grated	1 small onion, peeled and grated
salt	salt
freshly ground black pepper	freshly ground black pepper
1 × 275 g can condensed mushroom soup	1 × 10½ oz can condensed mushroom soup
2 × 15 ml spoons milk	2 tablespoons milk
300 ml water	½ pint water
little lemon juice	little lemon juice
a little freshly chopped mint	a little freshly chopped mint

H Pressure – 15 minutes

METHOD

Lightly grease a 1.2 litre/2 pint soufflé dish or other suitable size ovenproof dish with a little butter or margarine. Put half the potatoes in the bottom, add half the mushrooms and onion, a little salt and pepper, half the can of soup and 1 × 15 ml spoon/1 tablespoon of milk. Add the remaining ingredients in the same order. Cover with a piece of grease-proof paper. Put the water into the cooker with a little lemon juice. Stand the dish on the trivet, close cooker, bring to H pressure and cook for 15 minutes. Reduce the pressure quickly. Sprinkle with the mint before serving.

Ratatouille

METRIC	IMPERIAL
2 × 15 ml spoons olive oil	2 tablespoons olive oil
1 large onion, peeled and coarsely chopped	1 large onion, peeled and coarsely chopped
2 garlic cloves, crushed	2 garlic cloves, crushed
1 large aubergine, seeded and chopped	1 large aubergine, seeded and chopped
1 large green pepper, cored, seeded and sliced	1 large green pepper, cored, seeded and sliced
225 g courgettes, sliced	8 oz courgettes, sliced
225 g tomatoes, skinned, seeded and chopped or 1 × 400 g can tomatoes	8 oz tomatoes, skinned, seeded and chopped or 1 × 14 oz can tomatoes
300 ml water	½ pint water
salt	salt
freshly ground black pepper	freshly ground black pepper
To finish:	**To finish:**
1 × 5 ml spoon freshly chopped parsley	1 teaspoon freshly chopped parsley

Ratatouille; Scalloped potatoes and mushrooms

This rich vegetable stew comes from the Provence region of France. Although a stew it is usually eaten as an accompaniment to roasted or grilled meat or poultry. It also makes a delicious cold hors d'oeuvre.

H Pressure – 5 minutes

METHOD

Heat the oil in the cooker, add the onion and garlic and fry until they are beginning to colour. Add the aubergine and green pepper and fry for a few moments. Add all the remaining ingredients with a little salt and pepper and stir well. Close the cooker, bring to H pressure and cook for 5 minutes. Reduce the pressure quickly. If necessary, return the open cooker to the heat and cook rapidly for a few moments to reduce the liquid. Transfer to a serving dish and sprinkle with the parsley.

Cauliflower au gratin

Cauliflower au gratin

METRIC	IMPERIAL
1 medium cauliflower, leaves removed and washed	1 medium cauliflower, leaves removed and washed
300 ml hot water	½ pint hot water
salt	salt

To finish:

25 g butter or margarine	1 oz butter or margarine
1 × 15 ml spoon flour	1 tablespoon flour
150 ml milk	¼ pint milk
75 g Cheddar cheese, grated	3 oz Cheddar cheese, grated
freshly ground black pepper	freshly ground black pepper
1 × 15 ml spoon fresh white breadcrumbs	1 tablespoon fresh white breadcrumbs

H Pressure – 4 minutes

METHOD

Divide the cauliflower into quarters and remove the thick pieces of stalk. Put the water into the cooker and add the trivet, rim side down. Stand the cauliflower on the trivet and season lightly with salt. Close the cooker, bring to H pressure and cook for 4 minutes. Reduce the pressure quickly. Lift out the cauliflower and transfer to a lightly greased ovenproof dish. Drain off the liquid from the cooker, retaining 150 ml/¼ pint for the sauce.

Melt the butter or margarine in a small saucepan. Stir in the flour and cook gently for 1–2 minutes, stirring constantly. Remove the pan from the heat and gradually add the reserved cooking liquid and milk, stirring vigorously. Return the pan to the heat and bring to the boil, stirring constantly. Add 50 g/2 oz of the cheese and a little pepper, stir until the cheese has melted. Taste and adjust the seasoning of the sauce as necessary and pour the sauce evenly over the cooked cauliflower. Sprinkle the sauce with a mixture of the remaining cheese and breadcrumbs. Brown under a hot grill.

Vegetable and cheese pie

A tasty supper dish which can be made with any selection of vegetables.

METRIC	IMPERIAL
25 g butter or margarine	1 oz butter or margarine
1 onion, peeled and coarsely chopped	1 onion, peeled and coarsely chopped
1 green pepper, cored, seeded and chopped	1 green pepper, cored, seeded and chopped
4 stalks celery, scrubbed and coarsely chopped	4 stalks celery, scrubbed and coarsely chopped
100 g frozen or canned sweetcorn kernels	4 oz frozen or canned sweetcorn kernels
1 × 400 g can tomatoes, chopped	1 × 14 oz can tomatoes, chopped
1 × 5 ml spoon yeast extract e.g. Marmite	1 teaspoon yeast extract e.g. Marmite
150 ml hot brown stock or water and ¼ beef stock cube	¼ pint hot brown stock or water and ¼ beef stock cube

To finish:

175 g cheese, grated e.g. Cheddar, Lancashire	6 oz cheese, grated e.g. Cheddar, Lancashire
50 g fresh white breadcrumbs	2 oz fresh white breadcrumbs

H Pressure – 5 minutes

METHOD

Heat the butter or margarine in the cooker and lightly fry the onion, pepper and celery. Add the sweetcorn, tomatoes

with juice, yeast extract and stock or water and stock cube. Stir well. Close the cooker, bring to H pressure and cook for 5 minutes. Reduce the pressure quickly. Spoon half the mixture into a lightly greased ovenproof dish and cover with half the cheese. Add the remaining vegetables and then top with a mixture of the cheese and breadcrumbs. Brown and crisp the top under a hot grill or in the top of a hot oven.

Stuffed cabbage

METRIC	IMPERIAL
12 cabbage leaves	12 cabbage leaves
225 g cooked lamb, beef, chicken or ham, minced	8 oz cooked lamb, beef, chicken or ham, minced
1 small onion, peeled and grated	1 small onion, peeled and grated
50 g fresh white breadcrumbs	2 oz fresh white breadcrumbs
1 × 5 ml spoon freshly chopped parsley	1 teaspoon freshly chopped parsley
salt	salt
freshly ground black pepper	freshly ground black pepper
1 × 400 g can tomatoes, chopped	1 × 14 oz can tomatoes, chopped
300 ml hot brown stock or water and ½ beef stock cube	½ pint hot brown stock or water and ½ beef stock cube
1 × 15 ml spoon demerara sugar	1 tablespoon demerara sugar
2 × 5 ml spoons cornflour	2 teaspoons cornflour
little water	little water
chopped parsley (optional)	chopped parsley (optional)

H Pressure – 8 minutes

METHOD

Remove the thick white stem from each leaf and plunge the cabbage leaves into boiling salted water for 1 minute. Drain well. Mix together the meat, onion, breadcrumbs, parsley, salt and pepper. Spoon a little of the mixture on to the centre of each leaf, fold over edges of leaf and one end, then roll up to form a parcel, enclosing the filling. Put the tomatoes and their juice, stock or water and stock cube and sugar into the cooker and add the cabbage, seam side down. Close the cooker, bring to H pressure and cook for 8 minutes. Reduce the pressure quickly. Lift out the cabbage to a warmed dish and keep hot. Add the cornflour, blended with a little water to the sauce. Return the open cooker to the heat and bring to the boil, stirring constantly. Taste and adjust the seasoning and pour the sauce over the cabbage and garnish with a little chopped parsley, if liked.

Vegetable and cheese pie; Stuffed cabbage

Poultry and Game

Chicken is probably the poultry most commonly cooked. The advantage of a pressure cooker when cooking poultry, is that the older, tougher boiling fowls, which have so much flavour, can be cooked just as well as the roasting chicken. The only disadvantage is that a boiling fowl is rather larger than a roasting chicken and so may need to be cut in half or into portions to fit easily into the cooker. This is done to ensure that there is plenty of room left for a free circulation of steam.

Once it has been decided that the bird can be cooked whole, it should be trussed and tied into shape – this makes it much easier to handle, particularly if the bird is to be prebrowned. Any stuffing that is added must be calculated into the cooking time, which for whole birds is timed by the 500 g/1 lb.

All whole or portioned frozen poultry and game must be thoroughly thawed before cooking. This ensures that a safe internal cooking temperature is achieved, which cannot be guaranteed when cooking from a frozen state. With game birds such as pheasant or grouse the advantages of pressure cooking are that when the birds are getting a little older the flesh remains moist and tender. Wood pigeon and guinea fowl are seen increasingly in the shops and both of these can be substituted in several of the recipes which follow.

Timetable for poultry and game

POULTRY AND GAME	H (15 lb) PRESSURE	L (7½ lb) PRESSURE
CHICKEN		
Boiling fowl – whole	10–12 minutes per 500 g/1 lb	15–20 minutes per 500 g/1 lb (depending on age)
pieces	15 minutes	25 minutes
Roasting (broiler) – whole	8 minutes per 500 g/1 lb	12 minutes per 500 g/1 lb
pieces	5–6 minutes	10 minutes (depending on size)
Poussin (small roasting) –		
whole	8 minutes	12 minutes
DUCKLING – pieces	12–15 minutes	18–20 minutes (depending on size)
TURKEY – pieces	12–15 minutes	18–20 minutes (depending on size)
PHEASANT, GROUSE AND GUINEA FOWL –		
whole (young)	10–15 minutes	20–25 minutes
pieces (older)	20 minutes	30 minutes
PIGEONS – whole	15–20 minutes	25–30 minutes
RABBIT – whole	10 minutes per 500 g/1 lb	12 minutes per 500 g/1 lb
pieces	15–20 minutes	25–30 minutes (depending on age)
HARE – pieces	30 minutes	45 minutes

Chicken pot roast

A boiling fowl may be substituted for the roasting chicken in this recipe. Allow 10 minutes per 500 g/1 lb stuffed weight. Adjust the liquid accordingly (see liquid notes, page 11).

METRIC	IMPERIAL
75 g fresh white breadcrumbs	3 oz fresh white breadcrumbs
4 rashers unsmoked streaky bacon, rinded and chopped	4 rashers unsmoked streaky bacon, rinded and chopped
1 small onion, peeled and finely chopped	1 small onion, peeled and finely chopped
1 garlic clove, crushed	1 garlic clove, crushed
1 × 5 ml spoon dried thyme	1 teaspoon dried thyme
salt	salt
freshly ground black pepper	freshly ground black pepper
1 egg, beaten	1 egg, beaten
1.25 kg roasting chicken	2½ lb roasting chicken
50 g butter or margarine	2 oz butter or margarine
2 parsnips, peeled and quartered	2 parsnips, peeled and quartered
3 celery stalks, scrubbed and chopped	3 celery stalks, scrubbed and chopped
4 large carrots, peeled and quartered	4 large carrots, peeled and quartered
450 ml hot brown stock or water and 1 beef stock cube	¾ pint hot brown stock or water and 1 beef stock cube
2 × 15 ml spoons flour	2 tablespoons flour
little water	little water

Chicken pot roast

H Pressure – 25 minutes

METHOD

Mix together the breadcrumbs, bacon, onion, garlic, thyme and salt and pepper. Bind together with the beaten egg. Stuff the body cavity of the chicken with this mixture. Tie the chicken securely with fine string. Heat the butter or margarine in the base of the cooker and brown the chicken evenly all over. Remove the chicken and sauté the vegetables until lightly coloured. Transfer the vegetables to a plate. Add the hot stock or water and stock cube to the cooker and add the trivet. Stand the chicken on the trivet and add a little salt and pepper. Close the cooker, bring to H pressure and cook for 20 minutes. Reduce the pressure quickly.

Place the vegetables around the chicken, together with a little salt and pepper. Close the cooker, bring to H pressure and cook for 5 minutes. Reduce the pressure quickly. Lift out the chicken and vegetables to a warmed dish and keep hot. Remove the trivet and return the open cooker to the heat. Stir in the flour blended with a little water. Stir and cook until thickened. Taste and adjust seasoning as necessary before serving with the chicken.

Chicken and tomato casserole

Portions of boiling fowl may also be used for this recipe. Allow 15 minutes at H pressure.

METRIC	IMPERIAL
2 × 15 ml spoons oil	2 tablespoons oil
4 chicken portions or quarters, skinned	4 chicken portions or quarters, skinned
salt	salt
freshly ground black pepper	freshly ground black pepper
4 rashers unsmoked streaky bacon, rinded and chopped	4 rashers unsmoked streaky bacon, rinded and chopped
1 onion, peeled and sliced	1 onion, peeled and sliced
1 green pepper, cored, seeded and sliced	1 green pepper, cored, seeded and sliced
1 × 400 g can tomatoes	1 × 14 oz can tomatoes
150 ml white stock or water and ¼ chicken stock cube	¼ pint white stock or water and ¼ chicken stock cube
1 bay leaf	1 bay leaf
finely chopped parsley to garnish	finely chopped parsley to garnish

H Pressure – 6 minutes

METHOD

Heat the oil in the cooker. Season the chicken with salt and pepper. Fry with the bacon until the chicken is a light golden brown and the bacon is beginning to colour. Lift out of the cooker and drain well. Pour off any excess oil from the cooker. Add all the remaining ingredients to the cooker and return to the heat. Stir well to remove any residues from the base of the cooker. Return the chicken and bacon with a little more salt and pepper and stir well. Close the cooker, bring to H pressure and cook for 6 minutes. Reduce the pressure quickly. Remove the bay leaf before serving; taste and adjust seasoning as necessary and sprinkle with parsley.

Chicken with tarragon cream sauce

Chicken and tomato casserole; Chicken with tarragon cream sauce

METRIC	IMPERIAL
300 ml white stock	*½ pint white stock*
150 ml dry white wine	*¼ pint dry white wine*
4 chicken breast portions, skinned	*4 chicken breast portions, skinned*
salt	*salt*
freshly ground black pepper	*freshly ground black pepper*
1 × 5 ml spoon chopped fresh tarragon or 1 × 1.25 ml spoon dried	*1 teaspoon chopped tarragon or ½ teaspoon dried*

To finish:

beurre manié made with 40 g butter mixed with 1½ × 15 ml spoons flour
150 ml single cream
a little chopped fresh tarragon to garnish, if available

To finish:

beurre manié made with 1½ oz butter mixed with 1½ tablespoons flour
¼ pint single cream
a little chopped fresh tarragon to garnish, if available

H Pressure – 5 minutes

METHOD

Put the stock and wine into the cooker. Add the chicken with a little salt and pepper and the tarragon. Close the cooker, bring to H pressure and cook for 5 minutes. Reduce the pressure quickly. Lift out the chicken to a warmed serving dish, keep hot. Return the open cooker to the heat, add the beurre manié in small pieces, stirring constantly. Simmer until the sauce thickens. Taste and adjust seasoning as necessary. Remove the cooker from the heat, stir in the cream and pour the sauce over the chicken pieces. Sprinkle over chopped fresh tarragon, if available.

Eastern chicken

METRIC	IMPERIAL
25 g butter	1 oz butter
2 × 15 ml spoons cooking oil	2 tablespoons cooking oil
1 large onion, peeled and chopped	1 large onion, peeled and chopped
4 chicken portions or quarters, skinned	4 chicken portions or quarters, skinned
150 ml white stock or water and ½ chicken stock cube	¼ pint white stock or water and ½ chicken stock cube
150 ml medium dry sherry	¼ pint medium dry sherry
1 × 225 g can tomatoes	1 × 8 oz can tomatoes
2 × 5 ml spoons brown sugar	2 teaspoons brown sugar
2 × 5 ml spoons soy sauce	2 teaspoons soy sauce
2 oranges, peeled and segmented	2 oranges, peeled and segmented
salt	salt
freshly ground black pepper	freshly ground black pepper

To finish:

METRIC	IMPERIAL
2 × 5 ml spoons cornflour blended with 4 × 5 ml spoons water	2 teaspoons cornflour blended with 4 teaspoons water
orange slices	orange slices

H Pressure – 6 minutes

METHOD

Heat the butter and oil in the cooker. Fry the onion until it is beginning to soften. Lift out and drain well. Sauté the chicken portions until golden brown and lift out. Drain excess butter and oil from the cooker. Away from the heat add the stock or water and stock cube, sherry and tomatoes. Stir well to remove any residues from the base of the cooker. Return the chicken to the cooker with the onion, sugar, soy sauce, orange segments and a little salt and pepper. Close the cooker, bring to H pressure and cook for 6 minutes. Reduce the pressure quickly.

Lift out the chicken to a warmed serving dish and keep hot. Return the cooker to the heat and add the blended cornflour. Cook, stirring constantly, until the sauce boils and thickens. Taste and adjust the seasoning as necessary. Pour the sauce over the chicken and garnish with orange slices.

Coq au vin

This classic dish is readily adapted to pressure cooking and is most impressive if guests arrive unexpectedly.

METRIC	IMPERIAL
2 × 15 ml spoons cooking oil	2 tablespoons cooking oil
25 g butter	1 oz butter
4 rashers unsmoked streaky bacon, rinded and chopped	4 rashers unsmoked streaky bacon, rinded and chopped
12 pickling onions, peeled	12 pickling onions, peeled
100 g button mushrooms, cleaned	4 oz button mushrooms, cleaned
4 chicken portions or quarters, skinned	4 chicken portions or quarters, skinned
2 × 15 ml spoons brandy	2 tablespoons brandy
300 ml red wine (Burgundy-type)	½ pint red wine (Burgundy-type)
150 ml white stock or water and ½ chicken stock cube	¼ pint white stock or water and ½ chicken stock cube
1 garlic clove, crushed	1 garlic clove, crushed
1 bouquet garni	1 bouquet garni
salt	salt
freshly ground black pepper	freshly ground black pepper

To finish:
beurre manié made with
  25 g butter mixed with
  2 × 15 ml spoons flour

To finish:
beurre manié made with
  1 oz butter mixed with
  2 tablespoons flour

H Pressure – 6 minutes

METHOD

Heat the oil and butter in the cooker. Fry the bacon, onions and mushrooms until just beginning to colour. Lift out and drain well. Add the chicken and brown on both sides. Warm the brandy in a small saucepan, pour over the chicken and set alight. When the flames have died down return the bacon, onions and mushrooms to the cooker together with the wine, stock or water and stock cube, garlic, bouquet garni, salt and pepper. Stir well to remove any residues from the base of the cooker. Close the cooker, bring to H pressure and cook for 6 minutes.

Reduce the pressure quickly. Lift out the chicken and vegetables and keep hot. Remove the bouquet garni. Return the open cooker to the heat. Add the beurre manié in small pieces, stirring constantly, simmer until the sauce thickens. Taste and adjust the seasoning as necessary and serve the sauce poured over the chicken.

Coq au vin; Chicken, mushroom and pepper pie; Eastern chicken

Chicken, mushroom and pepper pie

For this recipe the pressure cooker greatly reduces the cooking time of the filling which, with a pastry lid, is finished in the oven.

METRIC	IMPERIAL
300 ml poultry stock or water and ½ chicken stock cube	*½ pint poultry stock or water and ½ chicken stock cube*
3 chicken portions, skinned	*3 chicken portions, skinned*
1 small green pepper, cored, seeded and sliced	*1 small green pepper, cored, seeded and sliced*
100 g small button mushrooms, cleaned	*4 oz small button mushrooms, cleaned*
salt	*salt*
freshly ground black pepper	*freshly ground black pepper*
1 bay leaf	*1 bay leaf*
few sprigs of fresh parsley	*few sprigs of fresh parsley*
few sprigs of fresh thyme or large pinch dried	*few sprigs of fresh thyme or large pinch dried*
Sauce:	**Sauce:**
25 g butter or margarine	*1 oz butter or margarine*
25 g flour	*1 oz flour*
approx. 150 ml milk	*approx. ¼ pint milk*
Pastry:	**Pastry:**
1 × 212 g packet frozen puff pastry, thawed	*1 × 7½ oz packet frozen puff pastry, thawed*
1 egg, beaten, to glaze	*1 egg, beaten, to glaze*

Pie Filling: H Pressure – 5 minutes
Pie Crust: Oven – 220°C, 425°F or Gas Mark 7

METHOD

Put the stock or water and stock cube, chicken, green pepper, mushrooms, salt and pepper and the herbs into the cooker. Close the cooker, bring to H pressure and cook for 5 minutes. Reduce the pressure quickly. Lift out the chicken and vegetables. Strain the cooking liquid into a measuring jug and make up to 450 ml/¾ pint with the milk for the sauce. Discard the bay leaf and herbs. Remove the chicken flesh from the bones and cut into 2.5 cm/1 inch pieces.

Melt the butter or margarine in the rinsed and dried cooker. Stir in the flour and cook gently for 1–2 minutes, stirring constantly. Remove the cooker from the heat and gradually add the cooking liquid and milk. Return the cooker to the heat and bring to the boil. Cook for 2 minutes, stirring constantly. Taste and adjust seasoning as necessary. Put the chicken and vegetables into a 900 ml/1½ pint pie dish and add the sauce. Roll out the pastry to fit the top of the pie dish, cutting a strip to go around the lip of the dish. Wet the lip and press the strip of pastry on. Wet the strip and cover with the pastry lid, trim if necessary and seal well. Make a steam hole in the centre of the pie. Decorate the top with leaves made from pastry trimmings and brush with beaten egg. Bake in a hot oven for 20 to 25 minutes or until the pastry is golden brown.

Galantine of chicken

METRIC	IMPERIAL
1.5–2 kg chicken	3–4 lb chicken
Stuffing:	**Stuffing:**
350 g pork sausagemeat	12 oz pork sausagemeat
1 × 5 ml spoon chopped fresh parsley	1 teaspoon chopped fresh parsley
1 × 5 ml spoon chopped fresh thyme	1 teaspoon chopped fresh thyme
1 × 5 ml spoon chopped fresh tarragon	1 teaspoon chopped fresh tarragon
1 × 5 ml spoon finely grated lemon rind	1 teaspoon finely grated lemon rind
salt	salt
freshly ground black pepper	freshly ground black pepper
100 g button mushrooms, washed and sliced	4 oz button mushrooms, washed and sliced
900 ml poultry stock or water and 1 chicken stock cube	1½ pints poultry stock or water and 1 chicken stock cube

Galantine of chicken

H Pressure – 10 minutes per 500 g/1 lb stuffed weight

METHOD

Bone the chicken or ask your butcher to do this for you. Lay the chicken on a board, skin side down and level the flesh as much as possible. Mix the sausagemeat with the herbs, lemon rind, salt and pepper. Spread half the sausagemeat mixture down the centre of the chicken and sprinkle with a little salt and pepper. Add a layer of the mushrooms and spread the remaining sausagemeat over the mushrooms, sprinkle with a little salt and pepper. Fold in the ends of the chicken first then fold over the longer edges so that the stuffing is well enclosed. Sew up with strong thread and weigh the chicken to calculate the cooking time. Wrap and tie securely into a pudding cloth or several thicknesses of muslin.

Put the stock into the cooker with the chicken. Close the cooker, bring to H pressure and cook for the calculated time. Reduce the pressure slowly. Lift out the chicken and reserve 300 ml/½ pint of the stock. Cool the chicken quickly and thoroughly. When quite cold, remove the cloth and thread carefully. Boil the reserved stock in a saucepan until well reduced and syrupy then cool. Brush the stock over the chicken. Transfer carefully to a serving dish and decorate the galantine with salad ingredients.

Curried chicken drumsticks with rice

This is a quickly prepared curry using basic curry ingredients, yet achieving the authentic hot and spicy flavour.

Curried chicken drumsticks with rice

METRIC	IMPERIAL
25 g butter or margarine	1 oz butter or margarine
1 onion, peeled and roughly chopped	1 onion, peeled and roughly chopped
2 × 15 ml spoons curry powder	2 tablespoons curry powder
1 × 5 ml spoon ground ginger	1 teaspoon ground ginger
1 × 2.5 ml spoon chilli powder	$\frac{1}{2}$ teaspoon chilli powder
450 ml hot white stock or water and $\frac{1}{2}$ chicken stock cube	$\frac{3}{4}$ pint hot white stock or water and $\frac{1}{2}$ chicken stock cube
8 chicken drumsticks, skinned	8 chicken drumsticks, skinned
1 garlic clove, crushed	1 garlic clove, crushed
1 eating apple, peeled and chopped	1 eating apple, peeled and chopped
25 g sultanas	1 oz sultanas
grated rind and juice of 1 lemon	grated rind and juice of 1 lemon
225 g long-grain patna rice	8 oz long-grain patna rice
450 ml water	$\frac{3}{4}$ pint water
1 × 2.5 ml spoon salt	$\frac{1}{2}$ teaspoon salt
1 × 15 ml spoon cornflour	1 tablespoon cornflour
little water	little water

H Pressure – 5 minutes

METHOD

Heat the butter or margarine in the base of the cooker. Fry the onion until lightly coloured. Stir in the curry powder, ginger and chilli powder. Remove the cooker from the heat and gradually stir in the stock or water and stock cube. Add all the remaining ingredients, except the rice, water, salt and cornflour and stir well. Place the trivet over the chicken. Put the rice, water and salt into an ovenproof dish that will fit easily into the cooker. Cover with a piece of greaseproof paper or foil. Stand the container on the trivet. Close the cooker, bring to H pressure and cook for 5 minutes. Reduce the pressure slowly. Lift out the container, transfer the rice to a strainer and rinse with boiling water. Drain well. Blend the cornflour with a little water and stir into the curry sauce. Return the open cooker to the heat and bring to the boil, stirring constantly. Taste and adjust the seasonings of the curry, as necessary, before serving on the bed of rice.

Braised fowl

The size of your pressure cooker may not allow you to cook a boiling chicken whole, as they are usually larger than the oven roasting variety. For ease of handling and serving, ask your butcher to joint it for you.

METRIC	IMPERIAL
1 thick slice unsmoked bacon, rinded and chopped	1 thick slice unsmoked bacon, rinded and chopped
25 g butter or margarine (optional)	1 oz butter or margarine (optional)
2 onions, peeled and sliced	2 onions, peeled and sliced
2 carrots, scraped and sliced	2 carrots, scraped and sliced
3 celery stalks, scrubbed and chopped	3 celery stalks, scrubbed and chopped
1 boiling fowl, jointed and skinned (if liked)	1 boiling fowl, jointed and skinned (if liked)
450 ml hot brown stock or water and ½ chicken stock cube	¾ pint hot brown stock or water and ½ chicken stock cube
1 × 15 ml spoon tomato purée	1 tablespoon tomato purée
salt	salt
freshly ground black pepper	freshly ground black pepper
1 bouquet garni	1 bouquet garni
To garnish:	**To garnish:**
grilled bacon rolls	grilled bacon rolls

H Pressure – 15 minutes

METHOD

Heat the cooker gently. Heat the bacon rind gently to release the fat. Add the bacon to the cooker and fry until beginning to colour. If necessary add the butter or margarine to the cooker and sauté the vegetables. Lift them out and drain well, discard the bacon rind. Brown the pieces of fowl well on both sides. Lift out the fowl and drain off the excess fat. Add the stock and tomato purée to the cooker, stir well. Replace the vegetables and bacon. Put the pieces of fowl on top. Add salt and pepper and the bouquet garni. Close the cooker, bring to H pressure and cook for 15 minutes. Reduce the pressure quickly. Discard the bouquet garni. Skim off any excess fat. Taste and adjust the seasoning as necessary. Serve garnished with grilled bacon rolls.

Boiling fowl with parsley sauce

METRIC	IMPERIAL
1 boiling fowl, jointed if very large	1 boiling fowl, jointed if very large
cold water	cold water
a few black peppercorns	a few black peppercorns
1 small onion, peeled and quartered	1 small onion, peeled and quartered
1 bay leaf	1 bay leaf
bunch of mixed fresh herbs	bunch of mixed fresh herbs

Sauce:	Sauce:
25 g butter or margarine	1 oz butter or margarine
25 g flour	1 oz flour
150 ml milk	¼ pint milk
1 × 15 ml spoon finely chopped fresh parsley	1 tablespoon finely chopped fresh parsley
salt	salt
white pepper	white pepper
finely chopped parsley, to garnish	finely chopped parsley, to garnish

H Pressure – 12 minutes per 500 g/1 lb

METHOD

Weigh the fowl to calculate the cooking time and wash and dry thoroughly. Truss with string for ease of handling. Put the fowl into the cooker, without the trivet, and add the water to half fill the cooker. Bring to the boil and skim well. Place the peppercorns in a bag and crush lightly with a rolling pin. Add the onion, herbs and crushed peppercorns. Close the cooker, bring to H pressure and cook for the calculated time. Reduce the pressure quickly. Lift out the fowl, drain well and remove the string. Cut the fowl into serving portions, place on a warmed dish and keep hot. Strain the liquid, reserve 300 ml/½ pint and rinse and dry the cooker.

Melt the butter or margarine in the cooker, add the flour and cook gently for 1 minute, stirring well. Remove from the heat and gradually stir in the reserved cooking liquid and the milk. Return to the heat and bring to the boil, stirring constantly. Add the parsley and salt and pepper to taste. Pour over the fowl and garnish with chopped parsley. Serve with plain boiled rice or buttered boiled potatoes.

Boiling fowl with parsley sauce; Braised fowl; Cheese topped chicken

Cheese topped chicken

If you wish to use quarters of chicken instead of chicken breasts allow 6 to 8 minutes cooking time, depending on the size.

METRIC
450 ml poultry stock or water and ½ chicken stock cube
1 bay leaf
1 small onion, finely chopped
4 breasts of chicken, skinned
salt
freshly ground black pepper
To finish:
25 g butter
25 g flour
75 g finely grated Parmesan cheese
50 g fresh white breadcrumbs

IMPERIAL
¾ pint poultry stock or water and ½ chicken stock cube
1 bay leaf
1 small onion, finely chopped
4 breasts of chicken, skinned
salt
freshly ground black pepper
To finish:
1 oz butter
1 oz flour
3 oz finely grated Parmesan cheese
2 oz fresh white breadcrumbs

H Pressure – 5 minutes

METHOD
Put the stock or water and stock cube, bay leaf, onion and chicken into the cooker, with a little salt and pepper. Close the cooker, bring to H pressure and cook for 5 minutes. Reduce the pressure quickly. Lift out the chicken and transfer to a warmed shallow flameproof dish, keep hot. Drain off and reserve the stock and discard the bay leaf. Rinse and dry the cooker.

Melt the butter in the cooker, stir in the flour and cook gently for 1 minute. Remove from the heat and gradually add the reserved stock. Return to the heat and bring to the boil, stirring constantly. Add 50 g/2 oz of the Parmesan cheese to the sauce with a little salt and pepper. Pour over the chicken. Mix together the breadcrumbs and remaining cheese, sprinkle liberally over the sauce and brown under a preheated hot grill. Serve hot.

METHOD

Heat the butter and oil in the cooker and sauté the onion until soft and transparent. Add the duck and brown evenly all over. Carefully drain off the butter and oil. Add the cider, salt and pepper and sugar, stir well. Close the cooker, bring to H pressure and cook for 15 minutes. Reduce the pressure quickly. Lift out the duck to a warmed dish and keep hot. Add the apples and cornflour, blended with a little water, to the sauce. Cook, stirring constantly until the sauce has thickened, simmer for 1 minute. Taste and adjust the seasoning as necessary before pouring the sauce over the duck. Garnish with a little chopped parsley to serve.

Braised orange duck

METRIC	IMPERIAL
50 g butter	2 oz butter
4 duck portions, trimmed	4 duck portions, trimmed
1 onion, peeled and sliced	1 onion, peeled and sliced
450 ml white stock or water and ½ chicken stock cube	¾ pint white stock or water and ½ chicken stock cube
2 oranges, rind thinly removed and cut into thin strips	2 oranges, rind thinly removed and cut into thin strips
1 tablespoon brown sugar	1 tablespoon brown sugar
juice of 2 oranges	juice of 2 oranges
salt	salt
freshly ground black pepper	freshly ground black pepper
beurre manié made with 25 g butter mixed with 1 × 15 ml spoon flour	beurre manié made with 1 oz butter mixed with 1 tablespoon flour
To garnish:	**To garnish:**
orange slices	orange slices
a little watercress	a little watercress

H Pressure – 15 minutes

METHOD

Heat the butter in the cooker. Prick the duck portions well and brown on both sides in the butter. Add the onion and cook until transparent. Lift out the duck and onion and drain well. Drain off excess fat from the cooker. Pour in the stock or water and stock cube with the orange rind, brown sugar and onion, stir well to remove any residues from the base of the cooker. Add the trivet, rim side down, and stand the duck pieces on top. Cover with the orange juice and a little salt and pepper. Close the cooker, bring to H pressure and cook for 15 minutes. Reduce the pressure quickly. Lift out the duck to a warmed serving dish, keep hot. Remove the trivet, skim the liquid of any fat and return to the heat. Add the beurre manié, in small pieces to the sauce, and stir constantly. Simmer until the sauce thickens. Taste and adjust the seasoning as necessary before pouring some of the sauce over the duck. Garnish with the orange slices and a little watercress and serve the remaining sauce separately.

Somerset duck casserole

Somerset duck casserole

METRIC	IMPERIAL
25 g butter	1 oz butter
2 × 15 ml spoons cooking oil	2 tablespoons cooking oil
1 large onion, peeled and chopped	1 large onion, peeled and chopped
4 duck portions, skinned if liked	4 duck portions, skinned if liked
450 ml dry cider	¾ pint dry cider
salt	salt
freshly ground black pepper	freshly ground black pepper
1 × 15 ml spoon demerara sugar	1 tablespoon demerara sugar
2 dessert apples, peeled, cored and chopped	2 dessert apples, peeled, cored and chopped
2 × 5 ml spoons cornflour	2 teaspoons cornflour
little water	little water
finely chopped parsley, to garnish	finely chopped parsley, to garnish

Country-style rabbit

METRIC

25 g butter or margarine
1 small rabbit, jointed
salt
freshly ground black pepper
1 onion, peeled and sliced
4 stalks celery, scrubbed and
    chopped
1 × 400 g can tomatoes
150 ml white stock or water
    and ½ chicken stock cube
1 × 15 ml spoon chopped
    parsley
2 × 5 ml spoons cornflour
1 × 15 ml spoon water
finely chopped parsley, to
    garnish

IMPERIAL

1 oz butter or margarine
1 small rabbit, jointed
salt
freshly ground black pepper
1 onion, peeled and sliced
4 stalks celery, scrubbed and
    chopped
1 × 14 oz can tomatoes
¼ pint white stock or water
    and ½ chicken stock cube
1 tablespoon chopped parsley
2 teaspoons cornflour
1 tablespoon water
finely chopped parsley, to
    garnish

H Pressure – 20 minutes

METHOD

Heat the butter or margarine in the cooker. Season the rabbit with salt and pepper and fry until a light golden brown on all sides. Lift out of the cooker and drain off any remaining butter or margarine. Add the remaining ingredients, except the cornflour and water to the cooker, and return to the heat. Stir well to remove any residues from the base of the cooker. Return the rabbit to the cooker and stir well. Close the cooker, bring to H pressure and cook for 20 minutes. Reduce the pressure quickly. Lift out the rabbit to a warmed dish and keep hot. Blend the cornflour with the water, stir into the sauce and bring to the boil, stirring well. Taste and adjust the seasoning as necessary before pouring the sauce over the rabbit. Garnish with a little chopped parsley.

Braised orange duck; Country-style rabbit

Rabbit with mustard cream sauce

METRIC
25 g butter or margarine
1 onion, peeled and sliced
1 small rabbit, jointed
2 × 5 ml spoons flour
2 × 5 ml spoons mustard
  powder
450 ml white stock or water
  and ½ chicken stock cube
salt

To finish:
1 × 2.5 ml spoon mustard
  powder
beurre manié made with
  25 g butter mixed with
  1 × 15 ml spoon flour
150 ml single cream

To garnish:
chopped chives

IMPERIAL
1 oz butter or margarine
1 onion, peeled and sliced
1 small rabbit, jointed
2 teaspoons flour
2 teaspoons mustard powder
¾ pint white stock or water
  and ½ chicken stock cube
salt

To finish:
½ teaspoon mustard powder
beurre manié made with
  1 oz butter mixed with
  1 tablespoon flour
¼ pint single cream

To garnish:
chopped chives

H Pressure – 20 minutes

METHOD
Heat the butter or margarine in the cooker and fry the onion until beginning to change colour. Lift out and drain well. Coat the rabbit pieces in a mixture of the flour and mustard powder and pat well onto the surface. Brown the rabbit in the hot butter or margarine. Lift out and drain off the excess butter or margarine from the cooker. Add the stock or water and stock cube to the cooker and stir well to remove any residues from the base of the cooker. Return the rabbit and onion to the cooker with a little salt. Close the cooker, bring to H pressure and cook for 20 minutes. Reduce the pressure quickly. Lift out the rabbit to a warmed serving dish and keep hot. Return the open cooker to the heat. Mix the mustard powder into the beurre manié and add small pieces to the liquid, stirring constantly. Simmer until the sauce thickens. Remove the cooker from the heat, stir in the cream and taste and adjust the seasoning as necessary before pouring the sauce over the rabbit. Sprinkle with chopped chives to serve and serve any extra sauce separately.

Brown rabbit stew

METRIC
25 g butter or margarine
1 large onion, peeled and
  sliced
4 large carrots, peeled and
  cut into 2.5 cm slices
2 parsnips, peeled and cut
  into 2.5 cm slices
4 rabbit portions
450 ml hot brown stock or
  water and ½ beef stock cube
1 bay leaf
salt
freshly ground black pepper

To finish:
2 × 15 ml spoons flour
little water
finely chopped parsley

IMPERIAL
1 oz butter or margarine
1 large onion, peeled and
  sliced
4 large carrots, peeled and
  cut into 1 inch slices
2 parsnips, peeled and cut
  into 1 inch slices
4 rabbit portions
¾ pint hot brown stock or
  water and ½ beef stock cube
1 bay leaf
salt
freshly ground black pepper

To finish:
2 tablespoons flour
little water
finely chopped parsley

H Pressure – 20 minutes

METHOD
Heat the butter or margarine in the base of the cooker. Fry the onion, carrots and parsnips until lightly browned. Remove from the cooker and drain well. Brown the rabbit in the hot butter or margarine and remove from the cooker. Away from the heat, add the stock or water and stock cube and stir well to remove any residues from the base of the cooker. Return the rabbit and vegetables to the cooker with the bay leaf and a little salt and pepper. Close the cooker, bring to H pressure and cook for 20 minutes. Reduce the pressure quickly. Transfer the rabbit and vegetables to a warmed serving dish and keep hot. Return the open cooker to the heat and stir in the flour blended with a little water. Cook, stirring constantly, until thickened. Taste and adjust the seasoning as necessary before pouring the sauce over the rabbit. Garnish with a little chopped parsley.

Braised hare with port

METRIC

4 rashers unsmoked streaky
bacon, rinds removed and
chopped
25 g butter or margarine
(optional)
1 large onion, peeled and
sliced
3 celery stalks, scrubbed and
chopped
1 hare, jointed
450 ml hot brown stock or
water and ½ beef stock cube
salt
freshly ground black pepper
1 bouquet garni

To finish:

3 × 15 ml spoons port
2 × 15 ml spoons redcurrant
jelly
2 × 5 ml spoons cornflour
little water
50 g button mushrooms,
cleaned
25 g butter

IMPERIAL

4 rashers unsmoked streaky
bacon, rinds removed and
chopped
1 oz butter or margarine
(optional)
1 large onion, peeled and
sliced
3 celery stalks, scrubbed and
chopped
1 hare, jointed
¾ pint hot brown stock or
water and ½ beef stock cube
salt
freshly ground black pepper
1 bouquet garni

To finish:

3 tablespoons port
2 tablespoons redcurrant jelly
2 teaspoons cornflour
little water
2 oz button mushrooms,
cleaned
1 oz butter

H Pressure – 30 minutes

METHOD

Heat the cooker gently. Cook the bacon rinds slowly before adding the chopped bacon. Add the butter or margarine if necessary and sauté the onion and celery until they are lightly browned. Lift out and drain well. Brown the pieces of hare in the hot fat. Lift out and drain off the excess fat. Add the hot stock or water and stock cube to the cooker. Make a bed of vegetables and place the pieces of hare on top, season with salt and pepper and add the bouquet garni. Close the cooker, bring to H pressure and cook for 30 minutes. Reduce the pressure quickly. Lift out the hare and vegetables to a warmed serving dish and keep hot. Discard the bouquet garni.

Return the open cooker to the heat, stir in the port, red-currant jelly and the cornflour, blended with a little water. Cook until boiling and thickened. Taste and adjust the seasoning as necessary. Pour the wine sauce over the hare and garnish with the mushrooms, which have been lightly sautéed in the butter.

Rabbit with mustard cream sauce; Brown rabbit stew; Braised hare with port

Pigeons in red wine

Pigeons in red wine

METRIC
50 g butter
4 pigeons, cleaned and trussed
12 pickling onions, peeled
*100 g mushrooms, cleaned
  and thickly sliced*
*300 ml red wine
  (Burgundy-type)*
*150 ml poultry stock or water
  and ½ chicken stock cube*
salt
freshly ground black pepper
1 × 2.5 ml spoon mixed herbs
*beurre manié made with
  25 g butter mixed with
  1 × 15 ml spoon flour*

To garnish:
freshly chopped parsley
finely grated rind of 1 lemon

IMPERIAL
2 oz butter
4 pigeons, cleaned and trussed
12 pickling onions, peeled
*4 oz mushrooms, cleaned and
  thickly sliced*
*½ pint red wine
  (Burgundy-type)*
*¼ pint poultry stock or water
  and ½ chicken stock cube*
salt
freshly ground black pepper
½ teaspoon mixed herbs
*beurre manié made with
  1 oz butter mixed with
  1 tablespoon flour*

To garnish:
freshly chopped parsley
finely grated rind of 1 lemon

H Pressure – 20 minutes

METHOD
Heat the butter in the cooker and brown the pigeons all over. Add the onions and mushrooms and sauté until both are beginning to colour. Add the wine, stock or water and stock cube, salt, pepper and herbs. Close the cooker, bring to H pressure and cook for 20 minutes. Reduce the pressure quickly. Lift out the pigeons and vegetables to a warmed dish and keep hot. Return the open cooker to the heat, add the beurre manié in small pieces stirring constantly until the sauce is thickened. Taste and adjust the seasoning as necessary. Pour a little sauce over the pigeons and sprinkle with a mixture of chopped parsley and lemon rind. Serve the remaining sauce separately.

Pheasant casserole

A young, small pheasant can be cooked whole allowing 10–15 minutes cooking time, however, for this style of casserole, older birds are excellent and should be halved or quartered.

METRIC
50 g butter
*100 g shallots or small
  onions, peeled*
*100 g button mushrooms,
  cleaned*
1 pheasant, jointed
*1 × 298 g can condensed
  consommé*
300 ml white stock or water
2 × 15 ml spoons sherry
*finely grated rind and juice of
  1 orange*
salt
freshly ground black pepper
orange slices for garnish

IMPERIAL
2 oz butter
*4 oz shallots or small
  onions, peeled*
*4 oz button mushrooms,
  cleaned*
1 pheasant, jointed
*1 × 10½ oz can condensed
  consommé*
½ pint white stock or water
2 tablespoons sherry
*finely grated rind and juice of
  1 orange*
salt
freshly ground black pepper
orange slices for garnish

H Pressure – 20 minutes

METHOD
Heat the butter in the cooker. Sauté the shallots and mushrooms until both are lightly browned. Lift out and drain well. Brown the pieces of pheasant all over. Lift out and drain off any excess butter from the cooker. Add the consommé, stock or water, sherry and orange rind and juice. Stir well to remove any residues from the base of the cooker. Return the vegetables and pheasant to the cooker with salt and pepper. Close the cooker, bring to H pressure and cook for 20 minutes. Reduce the pressure quickly. Lift out the pheasant and vegetables to a warmed dish and keep hot. Return the open cooker to the heat and boil quickly to reduce the liquid by approximately one-third. Taste and adjust the seasoning as necessary. Pour a little liquid over the pheasant and garnish with orange slices. Serve the remaining sauce separately.

Guinea fowl with grapes

METRIC	IMPERIAL
2 guinea fowl	2 guinea fowl
(allow ½ bird per person)	(allow ½ bird per person)
50 g butter	2 oz butter
100 g shallots or small	4 oz shallots or small
onions, peeled	onions, peeled
4 rashers unsmoked streaky	4 rashers unsmoked streaky
bacon, rinded	bacon, rinded
300 ml hot white stock or	½ pint hot white stock or
water and ½ chicken stock	water and ½ chicken stock
cube	cube
150 ml dry sherry	¼ pint dry sherry
100 g black grapes,	4 oz black grapes,
halved and pitted	halved and pitted
salt	salt
freshly ground black pepper	freshly ground black pepper
To finish:	**To finish**
2 × 5 ml spoons cornflour	2 teaspoons cornflour
little water	little water
a little fresh watercress	a little fresh watercress

H Pressure – 12 minutes

Guinea fowl with grapes; Pheasant casserole

METHOD

Wash and dry the birds thoroughly. Truss with string for ease of handling. Heat the butter in the cooker and brown the guinea fowl all over, lift out and drain well. Sauté the shallots in the hot butter, lift out then lightly fry the bacon. Lift out and drain off any excess butter from the cooker. Add the stock or water and stock cube and sherry to the cooker and stir well to remove any residues from the base of the cooker. Place the trivet, rim side down, in the cooker. Stand the guinea fowl on the trivet, and surround with the shallots and grapes. Sprinkle with a little salt and pepper and lay the bacon over the breast of the birds. Close the cooker, bring to H pressure and cook for 12 minutes. Reduce the pressure quickly. Lift out the guinea fowl and remove the string. Transfer to a warmed serving dish and surround with the shallots and grapes, keep hot.

Remove the trivet from the cooker and return the open cooker to the heat. Stir the cornflour, blended with a little water, into the stock. Bring to the boil, stirring continuously. Taste and adjust the seasoning of the sauce as necessary. Pour into a sauce boat to serve with the guinea fowl. Garnish the dish with fresh watercress just before serving.

Meat

The majority of dishes that make up our daily food fall into the categories of stews, casseroles, braises and pot roasts, with grilled prime meats and oven roasts becoming more and more the week-end or special occasion fare – the cost being a determining factor.

It is fortunate, therefore, that we have the pressure cooker, which is ideally suited to cook even the tougher cuts of meat, making them into a variety of tasty, tender dishes. The time saved is significant and coupled with this, the fuel savings become worthwhile.

The general methods of preparation for meats are little or no different to the oven or hotplate methods of cooking, but there are a few points which should be noted and which are reflected in the recipes that follow.

Stewing and casseroling

General instructions

1. For all recipes H (15 lb) pressure may be used, unless you own a cooker with a fixed L (7½ lb) pressure when the cooking times need to be increased by approximately half again.
2. The quantities given in each recipe are to serve four. If the quantity is increased or decreased the cooking time remains the same, as it is the size of the meat pieces that determines the time *not* the quantity.
3. The cooker should never be more than half full when all the ingredients and liquid have been added.
4. The trivet is only required if specifically mentioned. For the majority of dishes the food is placed straight into the base of the cooker.
5. Many recipes suggest pre-browning of the meats and vegetables, which is done in the open cooker over a low heat. After browning it is recommended that any excess fat is drained off and the cooking liquid added away from the heat and stirred well before returning the other ingredients to the cooker. This may seem a lengthy process but by doing this the frying residues are removed and will prevent catching or sticking on the cooker base.
6. Generally it is better to cook in a thin liquid, such as stock or wine, adjusting the consistency at the completion of cooking. Meats can be coated in flour before cooking but care should be taken to ensure that the liquid is not too thick before cooking commences, otherwise the flour can cause sticking to the base. In this case, the ingredients should be brought to the boil in the open cooker before pressure cooking and a little more stock added if necessary.

   Blended flour, cornflour or a *beurre manié* (equal quantities of butter and flour mixed to a paste) can be added after cooking finishes and are used to thicken the sauce in the open cooker, stirring well. Cream, soured cream or egg yolks can also be stirred in for added richness.
7. Pressure may always be lowered quickly unless specifically stated in a recipe.
8. Adjustments to your own recipes. It will often be found that, as there is little evaporation during cooking, less liquid may be required, but it should

never be less than 300 ml/½ pint. Seasonings, spices and herbs may need to be used more sparingly and it is a good idea to adjust seasoning after cooking.

9. If you wish to use meats other than those indicated in each recipe, or larger pieces, the cooking times will require adjustment accordingly.

Braising

By tradition, braising is the method of cooking where the meat is cooked on a bed of vegetables (a mirepoix) with a little liquid. Like stewing and casseroling it is readily adapted to the pressure cooker and either a mirepoix or the trivet lifts the meat out of the liquid.

Pot roasting

This method of cooking has many advantages, not least the opportunity of using the less expensive joints which you may otherwise overlook. Brisket, in particular, can be made into a variety of dishes adding flavour with wine, beer or vegetables. A pot roast will be cooked in a fraction of the time required by other methods and the result will always be moist, tender and succulent. Vegetables can be added part way through the cooking so that a main course can be completed in the one cooker. Prime cuts of meat can be pot-roasted but recipes are not included as it is felt that these are at their best when oven roasted.

General instructions

1. For the majority of cookers the joint should be no larger than 1.5 kg/3 lb and for ease of handling, should be tied into a neat shape with string.

2. All joints are timed by the 500 g/1 lb and the liquid *must* be increased to cover the cooking period. See notes on Liquids, page 11. The thickness of the joint should be taken into account as a thin joint will cook more quickly than a thicker one. A joint should have the weight calculated to include the stuffing.

3. The joint should be pre-browned in the base of the cooker before pressure cooking. A little flour dusted over the joint before cooking helps the browning and if this is not done, the joint should be thoroughly dried to prevent excessive splashing and spitting of the fat.

4. After browning, the joint should be removed from the cooker, the hot liquid added and the trivet placed in the base, rim side down. This lifts the meat away from the base of the cooker. The seasoned joint is then replaced and cooked for the recommended time, using H (15 lb) or L (7½ lb) pressure.

5. Pressure may always be lowered quickly, unless specifically stated in a recipe.

6. After cooking, the stock can be thickened with a little blended flour or blended cornflour in the open cooker or, if vegetables have been added for flavour, these can be mashed into the liquid to thicken it.

Timetable for pot roasting		
MEAT	TIME PER 500 g/1 lb	
	H (15 lb) PRESSURE	L (7½ lb) PRESSURE
Beef: Brisket – rolled	20 minutes	30 minutes
Silverside	15 minutes	20 minutes
Topside	12 minutes	18 minutes
Rump – rolled	12 minutes	18 minutes
Top ribs – boned and rolled	12 minutes	18 minutes
Lamb: Breast – boned and rolled	15 minutes	20 minutes
Shoulder – boned and rolled	15 minutes	20 minutes
Best end	12 minutes	18 minutes
Leg – boned and tied	12 minutes	18 minutes
Pork: Shoulder – boned and rolled	15 minutes	20 minutes
Loin	12 minutes	18 minutes
Leg – boned and tied	15 minutes	20 minutes
Veal: Breast – boned and rolled	10–12 minutes	20 minutes
Shoulder – boned and rolled	12–15 minutes	20 minutes
Knuckle and Oyster	12 minutes	18 minutes
Loin	10 minutes	15 minutes

Example for calculating cooking time and liquid at H (15 lb) pressure:
1 kg/2 lb joint of brisket
Cooking time required 40 minutes
Liquid required 600 ml/1 pint: 300 ml/½ pint for the first 15 minutes and an additional 150 ml/¼ pint for each additional 15 minutes.

Boiling

Meats most suitable for boiling are: brisket or silverside (boiled beef and dumplings for example); salted meats to be served hot or cold with salads; bacon, hams and tongues.

General instructions

1. Like pot roasting the cooking time is calculated by the 500 g/1 lb, but the amount of liquid used is far greater as the meat should be almost covered. However, when the meat and liquid have been added, the cooker should not be more than half full.

2. The trivet is not required as the meat should be in the liquid.

3. Salted meat, bacon, ham or tongue should be soaked in cold water for at least 4 hours before cooking and the soaking liquid discarded. Alternatively, the joint can be brought to the boil with sufficient water to cover. Stand for 5 minutes then drain and discard the water.

4. Before pressure cooking always bring the meat and

liquid to the boil in the open cooker and skim well.

5. Pressure can always be lowered quickly. If the meat is to be served cold it is a good idea to let the meat cool in the cooking liquid after reducing pressure. This keeps the meat moist and succulent.

Timetable for boiling

MEAT	TIME PER 500 g/1 lb	
	H (15 lb) PRESSURE	L (7½ lb) PRESSURE
Brisket	15 minutes	20–25 minutes
Silverside	15 minutes	20–25 minutes
Bacon and ham: prime cuts, middle and corner gammon	8–10 minutes	15 minutes
cheaper cuts, collar, forehock, slipper	12 minutes	18 minutes
Ox tongue	15 minutes	20–25 minutes
Lamb's tongues	20 minutes	30 minutes only

Boil-in-the-bag meats

Put the trivet into the cooker, rim side up, and stand the joint on the trivet. Add cold water to half fill the cooker. Bring to H pressure and cook for 14 minutes per 500 g/1 lb for bacon joints, and 12 minutes per 500 g/1 lb for gammon joints, reduce pressure quickly.

Cooking meats for the home freezer

The home freezer and a pressure cooker are two very compatible appliances. The pressure cooker gives speed of cooking, even for large quantities, and the home freezer gives the convenience of storage for prepared dishes. By using a pressure cooker, batch cooking need no longer be a day long exercise, indeed a few hours one evening may be all that is required to cook a selection of dishes. Alternatively, one can double the quantities when making a stew as the time it takes to prepare the extra ingredients is minimal.

When your cooking is intended for the freezer, the cooking time should be reduced by 2 to 3 minutes, as this will be made up at the reheating stage and will prevent overcooking. Also it is better *not* to thicken the sauce or gravy before freezing. You will see in the instructions below that a little liquid has to be added to the cooker for reheating the food from a frozen state and this will obviously thin the gravy. Therefore if the adjustment is left to the reheating stage it can be made to exactly the consistency you prefer.

Reheating frozen stews, casseroles, etc.

Put 150 ml/¼ pint water or stock into the cooker, without the trivet. Add the block of unwrapped food. Bring

to H (15 lb) pressure for 8 to 12 minutes or 12 to 15 minutes at L (7½ lb) pressure. Reduce the pressure quickly. Adjust the consistency of the gravy or sauce with a little blended flour or blended cornflour or boil rapidly for 2 to 3 minutes in the open cooker to evaporate some of the liquid. If you prefer to defrost the food before reheating, follow the same instructions as above but without the liquid and reheat for only 2 to 3 minutes at H (15 lb) or L (7½ lb) pressure.

Cooking raw meats from frozen

This is very much a matter of personal choice, but the advantage of using this method, if you have forgotten to defrost the meat, cannot be questioned.

Meats for stews or casseroles

If you intend using cubed or sliced meats for a dish, it is obviously better if the cutting up is done before freezing, as in this way the meat will separate as it cooks and will require no further handling.

Pre-browning

If the recipe requires the meat to be pre-browned do this in hot fat in the open cooker, over a low heat. Continue cooking, keeping the heat low, until the meat separates and begins to colour. Stir occasionally to aid this. Then add the hot liquid and continue cooking in the normal way adding 5 minutes to the recommended cooking time. Reduce the pressure quickly.

If the meat is not to be pre-browned, put the block of frozen meat into the cooker with 450 ml/¾ pint of hot stock, salt and pepper and vegetables. Bring to pressure and cook for 5 to 8 minutes longer than the recommended time. Reduce the pressure quickly.

Minced meat

This should be partially thawed and separated into smaller pieces if it is to be cooked from the raw state with no pre-browning. Place the meat with 300 ml/½ pint hot stock, salt and pepper and vegetables into the cooker and cook at H pressure for 10 minutes. Reduce pressure quickly. After cooking, stir thoroughly and adjust the consistency of the sauce. Alternatively, the block of meat can be pre-browned in the open cooker over a low heat, until it begins to soften and separate then proceed as above.

Joints

These should be pre-browned in hot fat in the open cooker. The heat should be kept low and cooking continued until the outside flesh has softened. For each of the joints listed under the pot-roasting timetable on page 72, add 10 minutes per 500 g/1 lb to the cooking time recommended and increase the liquid accordingly. Reduce the pressure quickly.

Meatballs in tomato sauce

METRIC	IMPERIAL
750 g minced beef	1½ lb minced beef
1 small onion, peeled and grated	1 small onion, peeled and grated
1 × 5 ml spoon mixed herbs	1 teaspoon mixed herbs
salt	salt
freshly ground black pepper	freshly ground black pepper
1 egg, beaten	1 egg, beaten
50 g lard or margarine	2 oz lard or margarine
1 × 400 g can tomatoes, chopped	1 × 14 oz can tomatoes, chopped
300 ml brown stock or water and ½ beef stock cube	½ pint brown stock or water and ½ beef stock cube
1 × 15 ml spoon Worcestershire sauce	1 tablespoon Worcestershire sauce
2 × 5 ml spoons cornflour	2 teaspoons cornflour
little water	little water
finely chopped parsley, to garnish	finely chopped parsley, to garnish

H Pressure – 8 minutes

METHOD

Mix together the minced beef, onion, herbs, salt and pepper. Bind with the beaten egg. Turn out on to a well-floured surface, divide the meat mixture into 12 pieces and shape into balls. Heat the lard or margarine in the cooker and brown the meatballs quickly and evenly. Lift out and drain the excess lard from the cooker. Add the tomatoes, stock or water and stock cube and Worcestershire sauce to the cooker and stir well to remove any residues from the base of the cooker. Return the meatballs to the cooker. Close the cooker, bring to H pressure and cook for 8 minutes. Reduce the pressure quickly. Return the open cooker to the heat, stir in the cornflour blended with a little water and cook until boiling and thickened, stirring constantly. Taste and adjust the seasoning as necessary and serve garnished with chopped parsley.

Beef loaf

METRIC	IMPERIAL
500 g minced beef	1 lb minced beef
1 small onion, peeled and finely chopped	1 small onion, peeled and finely chopped
2 rashers unsmoked streaky bacon, rinded and finely chopped	2 rashers unsmoked streaky bacon, rinded and finely chopped
75 g fresh white breadcrumbs	3 oz fresh white breadcrumbs
1 × 225 g can tomatoes, chopped	1 × 8 oz can tomatoes, chopped
1 × 15 ml spoon freshly chopped parsley	1 tablespoon freshly chopped parsley
salt	salt
freshly ground black pepper	freshly ground black pepper
1 egg, beaten	1 egg, beaten
450 ml water	¾ pint water
little lemon juice	little lemon juice
small bunch watercress, to garnish	small bunch watercress, to garnish

H Pressure – 30 minutes

METHOD

In a mixing bowl place the beef, onion, bacon, breadcrumbs, tomatoes and parsley and thoroughly combine. Add salt and pepper and bind the mixture with the beaten egg. Transfer the meat mixture to a seamless, lightly greased 500 g/1 lb loaf tin or other suitable size ovenproof dish. Press down well and cover with a double layer of greased greaseproof paper or a single layer of aluminium foil. Put the water into the cooker with a little lemon juice and the trivet, rim side down. Stand the dish on the trivet. Close the cooker, bring to H pressure and cook for 30 minutes. Reduce the pressure quickly. Garnish with watercress and serve hot with tomato sauce, potatoes and a green vegetable or cold with a mixed salad.

Variations:

The Beef loaf can have other ingredients added to enhance or completely change the basic taste. Combine with the basic mixture and cook as above.

Finely chopped mushrooms and a small green or red pepper, seeded and chopped are good additions. For a fruity mixture, add 25 g/1 oz sultanas. For a Chinese-style Beef loaf, add soy and chilli sauce to taste. Remember to season lightly with salt as soy sauce can be very salty. Serve with boiled rice.

Meatballs in tomato sauce

Cottage pie

METRIC	IMPERIAL
25 g lard or margarine	1 oz lard or margarine
1 onion, peeled and chopped	1 onion, peeled and chopped
2 carrots, scraped and coarsely grated	2 carrots, scraped and coarsely grated
50 g mushrooms, cleaned and chopped	2 oz mushrooms, cleaned and chopped
500 g minced beef	1 lb minced beef
300 ml hot brown stock or water and ½ beef stock cube	½ pint hot brown stock or water and ½ beef stock cube
salt	salt
freshly ground black pepper	freshly ground black pepper
750 g old potatoes, peeled and quartered if large	1½ lb old potatoes, peeled and quartered if large
25 g butter or margarine	1 oz butter or margarine
a little milk	a little milk
2 × 5 ml spoons cornflour for thickening	2 teaspoons cornflour for thickening

H Pressure – 6 minutes

METHOD

Melt the lard or margarine in the cooker. Fry the onion

Beef loaf; Cottage pie

until it begins to soften, add the carrots and mushrooms and cook for a few moments. Lift the vegetables out of the cooker and drain well. Brown the minced beef in the hot lard or margarine and then carefully drain the excess lard or margarine from the cooker. Add the hot stock or water and stock cube to the cooker, and stir well to remove any residues from the base of the cooker. Add salt, pepper and the vegetables to the beef. Cover the beef with the trivet. Place the lightly salted potatoes in a separator (if this is perforated line first with a piece of aluminium foil or grease-proof paper). Stand the separator on the trivet. Close the cooker, bring to H pressure on a medium heat and cook for 6 minutes. Reduce the pressure quickly.

Lift out the potatoes, transfer to a basin and mash with butter, salt, pepper and a little milk until they are smooth and creamy. Return the open cooker to the heat and add the cornflour blended with a little water. Cook, stirring constantly, until thickened. Taste and adjust the seasoning as necessary. Transfer the meat to a 1.2 litre/2 pint flameproof dish. Top with the mashed potato, marking a pattern on the top with a fork. Brown under a hot grill and serve with a green vegetable.

75

Beef in Burgundy

METRIC	IMPERIAL
25 g butter	1 oz butter
2 × 15 ml spoons cooking oil	2 tablespoons cooking oil
1 large onion, peeled and sliced	1 large onion, peeled and sliced
750 g stewing beef, trimmed and cubed	1½ lb stewing beef, trimmed and cubed
300 ml red wine (Burgundy-type)	½ pint red wine (Burgundy-type)
1 × 400 g can tomatoes	1 × 14 oz can tomatoes
100 g button mushrooms, cleaned	4 oz button mushrooms, cleaned
salt	salt
freshly ground black pepper	freshly ground black pepper
bouquet garni	bouquet garni

To finish:

1–2 × 15 ml spoons flour blended with 2 × 15 ml spoons water	1–2 tablespoons flour blended with 2 tablespoons water
a little chopped fresh parsley	a little chopped fresh parsley

H Pressure – 20 minutes

METHOD

Heat the butter and oil in the cooker. Fry the onion until lightly browned. Lift out and drain well. Sauté the beef in the butter and oil until well browned all over. Lift out and drain the excess butter and oil from the cooker. Away from the heat, add the wine and tomatoes to the cooker. Stir well to remove any residues from the base of the cooker. Return the meat and onion to the cooker with the mushrooms, salt and pepper and the bouquet garni. Close the cooker, bring to H pressure and cook for 20 minutes. Reduce the pressure quickly and remove the bouquet garni. Return the open cooker to the heat and add the blended flour, stirring constantly. Bring to the boil and simmer for 1 minute. Taste and adjust the seasoning as necessary. Serve sprinkled with the chopped parsley.

Continental pot roast

METRIC	IMPERIAL
50 g lard or margarine	2 oz lard or margarine
1 large onion, peeled and sliced	1 large onion, peeled and sliced
1 garlic clove, crushed	1 garlic clove, crushed
1 kg piece of topside of beef	2 lb piece of topside of beef
300 ml Beaujolais	½ pint Beaujolais
150 ml brown stock or water and ½ beef stock cube	¼ pint brown stock or water and ½ beef stock cube
salt	salt
freshly ground black pepper	freshly ground black pepper
1 × 400 g can tomatoes	1 × 14 oz can tomatoes
1 bay leaf	1 bay leaf
1 × 15 ml spoon cornflour	1 tablespoon cornflour
a little cold water	a little cold water
100 g black olives, stoned	4 oz black olives, stoned

Carbonnade of beef; Continental pot roast; Beef in burgundy

H Pressure – 25 minutes

METHOD

Heat the lard or margarine in the cooker, add the onion and garlic, and fry until light golden brown. Lift out and drain well. Brown the beef well on all sides, lift out and drain off excess lard or margarine from the cooker. Pour the Beaujolais and stock or water and stock cube into the cooker and stir well to remove any residues from the base of the cooker. Put the trivet into the cooker, rim side down. Stand the beef on the trivet and season well with salt and pepper. Put the onion, garlic and tomatoes around the meat with the bay leaf. Close the cooker, bring to H pressure and cook for 25 minutes. Reduce the pressure quickly. Lift out the beef and discard the bay leaf. Remove the trivet from the cooker. Blend the cornflour with a little cold water and stir into the liquid. Bring to the boil, stirring constantly, then simmer for 1 minute. Add the olives to the sauce. Taste and adjust the seasoning as necessary before serving around the meat.

Carbonnade of beef

METRIC

25 g lard or margarine
1 large onion, peeled and
 sliced
2 garlic cloves, crushed
750 g stewing beef, trimmed
 and cubed
300 ml brown ale
300 ml brown stock or water
 and ½ beef stock cube
salt
freshly ground black pepper
2 bay leaves

To finish:
beurre manié made with
 25 g butter mixed with
 1 × 15 ml spoon flour
French bread, cut into thick
 slices
Dijon mustard

IMPERIAL

1 oz lard or margarine
1 large onion, peeled and
 sliced
2 garlic cloves, crushed
1½ lb stewing beef, trimmed
 and cubed
½ pint brown ale
½ pint brown stock or water
 and ½ beef stock cube
salt
freshly ground black pepper
2 bay leaves

To finish:
beurre manié made with
 1 oz butter mixed with
 1 tablespoon flour
French bread, cut into thick
 slices
Dijon mustard

H Pressure – 20 minutes

METHOD

Heat the lard or margarine in the cooker. Fry the onion and garlic until well browned. Lift out and drain well. Sauté the beef until well browned all over. Lift out and drain off the excess lard or margarine from the cooker. Away from the heat, add the brown ale and stock or water and stock cube. Stir well to remove any residues from the base of the cooker. Return the meat, onion and garlic to the cooker with some salt and pepper and the bay leaves. Close the cooker, bring to H pressure and cook for 20 minutes. Reduce the pressure quickly. Return the open cooker to the heat and add the beurre manié in small pieces, stirring constantly. Simmer until the sauce thickens. Taste and adjust the seasoning as necessary and transfer the meat to a flameproof dish.

Spread one side of the French bread with a little Dijon mustard. Arrange the bread, mustard side up, over the meat and press each slice into the sauce. Place under a hot grill for a few moments until the bread is heated through and beginning to turn golden brown.

Mexican beef casserole

METRIC	IMPERIAL
50 g lard or margarine	2 oz lard or margarine
1 large onion, peeled and sliced	1 large onion, peeled and sliced
1 large green pepper, cored, seeded and sliced	1 large green pepper, cored, seeded and sliced
750 g stewing beef, trimmed and cubed	1½ lb stewing beef, trimmed and cubed
25 g flour	1 oz flour
salt	salt
freshly ground black pepper	freshly ground black pepper
1 × 5 ml spoon chilli powder	1 teaspoon chilli powder
300 ml hot brown stock or water and ½ beef stock cube	½ pint hot brown stock or water and ½ beef stock cube
1 × 400 g can tomatoes	1 × 14 oz can tomatoes
100 g packet frozen sweetcorn kernels	4 oz packet frozen sweetcorn kernels

H Pressure – 20 minutes

METHOD
Heat the lard or margarine in the cooker, add the onion and pepper and fry until both are beginning to colour. Lift out and drain well. Coat the meat in flour seasoned with salt and pepper. Brown the meat in the hot lard or margarine, lift out and drain well. Stir the chilli powder into the cooking juices, add the hot stock or water and stock cube and stir well to remove any residues from the base of the cooker. Return the meat and vegetables to the cooker together with the tomatoes and sweetcorn. Stir and bring to the boil. If the liquid is too thick add a little more water to the cooker. Close the cooker, bring to H pressure and cook for 20 minutes. Reduce the pressure quickly. Stir well, taste and adjust the seasoning as necessary, serve with pasta or rice.

Brisket in beer

METRIC	IMPERIAL
25 g lard or margarine	1 oz lard or margarine
1 kg piece of rolled brisket of beef	2 lb piece of rolled brisket of beef
1 large onion, peeled and sliced	1 large onion, peeled and sliced
2 large carrots, scraped and sliced	2 large carrots, scraped and sliced
600 ml brown ale	1 pint brown ale
salt	salt
freshly ground black pepper	freshly ground black pepper
bouquet garni	bouquet garni

H Pressure – 40 minutes

METHOD
Heat the lard or margarine in the cooker. Brown the beef well on all sides, lift out and drain well. Fry the vegetables until lightly coloured. Lift out and drain well. Away from the heat add the brown ale to the cooker. Stir well to remove any residues from the base of the cooker. Stand the trivet in the cooker, rim side down. Place the browned beef on the trivet with the vegetables surrounding the meat. Season lightly with salt and pepper and add the bouquet garni. Close the cooker, bring to H pressure and cook for 40 minutes. Reduce the pressure quickly. Lift out the joint and discard the bouquet garni. Remove the strings from the meat and carve into thick slices. Remove the trivet from the cooker and mash the vegetables into the liquid. Taste and adjust the seasoning of the sauce as necessary before pouring over the meat.

Mexican beef casserole; Brisket in beer; Chilli con carne

Chilli con carne

METRIC	IMPERIAL
100 g red kidney beans	*4 oz red kidney beans*
boiling water	*boiling water*
2 × 15 ml spoons cooking oil	*2 tablespoons cooking oil*
1 large onion, peeled and chopped	*1 large onion, peeled and chopped*
1 garlic clove, crushed	*1 garlic clove, crushed*
500 g minced beef	*1 lb minced beef*
1 × 5 ml spoon chilli powder	*1 teaspoon chilli powder*
1 × 400 g can tomatoes	*1 × 14 oz can tomatoes*
300 ml hot brown stock or water and ½ beef stock cube	*½ pint hot brown stock or water and ½ beef stock cube*
1 × 15 ml spoon tomato purée	*1 tablespoon tomato purée*
salt	*salt*

H Pressure – 12 minutes

METHOD

Place the beans in a large basin. Cover with boiling water and leave to stand for at least 2 hours. Heat the oil in the cooker, add the onion and garlic and fry until both are beginning to colour. Add the minced beef and fry lightly. Drain off any excess oil from the cooker. Stir in the chilli powder, tomatoes, stock or water and stock cube, tomato purée, salt to taste and the drained kidney beans. Close the cooker, bring to H pressure and cook for 12 minutes. Reduce the pressure slowly. Adjust the seasoning and consistency as necessary. Serve on a bed of boiled rice.

Beef and bean casserole

METRIC

75 g haricot beans
boiling water
50 g lard or margarine
1 large onion, peeled and
  sliced
2 carrots, peeled and sliced
500 g shin of beef, trimmed
  and cubed
600 ml hot brown stock or
  water and ½ beef stock cube
2 × 15 ml spoons tomato
  purée
salt
freshly ground black pepper
1 bay leaf
2 × 5 ml spoons cornflour
a little cold water
finely chopped parsley, to
  garnish

IMPERIAL

3 oz haricot beans
boiling water
2 oz lard or margarine
1 large onion, peeled and
  sliced
2 carrots, peeled and sliced
1 lb shin of beef, trimmed
  and cubed
1 pint hot brown stock or
  water and ½ beef stock cube
2 tablespoons tomato purée
salt
freshly ground black pepper
1 bay leaf
2 teaspoons cornflour
a little cold water
finely chopped parsley, to
  garnish

H Pressure – 20 minutes

METHOD

Put the haricot beans into a basin, cover with boiling water and leave to stand for 1 hour. Melt the lard or margarine in the cooker. Add the onion and carrots and fry until lightly coloured. Add the meat and sauté until evenly browned. Remove the cooker from the heat, stir in the stock or water and stock cube, tomato purée, salt, pepper, bay leaf and the drained haricot beans. Return to the heat and bring to the boil. Close the cooker, bring to H pressure and cook for 20 minutes. Reduce the pressure slowly. Remove the bay leaf and add the cornflour, blended with a little cold water. Bring to the boil, stirring constantly and simmer for 1 minute. Taste and adjust the seasoning as necessary and sprinkle with a little chopped parsley to serve.

Braised beef with peppers

METRIC

50 g lard or margarine
1 onion, peeled and sliced
2 red peppers, cored, seeded
  and sliced
750 g chuck steak, cut into
  four 2.5 cm thick slices
450 ml hot brown stock or
  water and ½ beef stock cube
100 g sweetcorn kernels
salt
freshly ground black pepper

IMPERIAL

2 oz lard or margarine
1 onion, peeled and sliced
2 red peppers, cored, seeded
  and sliced
1½ lb chuck steak, cut into
  four 1 inch thick slices
¾ pint hot brown stock or
  water and ½ beef stock cube
4 oz sweetcorn kernels
salt
freshly ground black pepper

H Pressure – 20 minutes

METHOD

Heat the lard or margarine in the cooker and sauté the onion and peppers until both are beginning to soften. Lift out and drain well. Brown the meat on both sides in the hot lard or margarine. Lift out and drain off the excess lard or margarine

from the cooker. Add the stock or water and stock cube to the cooker and stir well to remove any residues from the base of the cooker. Put the vegetables and sweetcorn into the cooker, place the meat slices on top and season with salt and pepper. Close the cooker, bring to H pressure and cook for 20 minutes. Reduce the pressure quickly. Taste and adjust the seasoning as necessary before serving.

Beef roulades

METRIC	IMPERIAL
750 g topside of beef, thinly sliced and beaten	1½ lb topside of beef, thinly sliced and beaten
salt	salt
freshly ground black pepper	freshly ground black pepper
75 g fresh white breadcrumbs	3 oz fresh white breadcrumbs
1 × 5 ml spoon mixed herbs	1 teaspoon mixed herbs
50 g mushrooms, cleaned and chopped	2 oz mushrooms, cleaned and chopped
1 small onion, peeled and grated	1 small onion, peeled and grated
1 egg, beaten	1 egg, beaten
25 g lard or margarine	1 oz lard or margarine
300 ml brown stock or water and ½ beef stock cube	½ pint brown stock or water and ½ beef stock cube
300 ml red wine (Burgundy-type)	½ pint red wine (Burgundy-type)
2 × 15 ml spoons flour	2 tablespoons flour
little water	little water
a little freshly chopped parsley	a little freshly chopped parsley

H Pressure – 25 minutes

METHOD

Divide the meat into portions and season lightly with salt and pepper. For the stuffing, mix together the breadcrumbs, herbs, mushrooms, onion, salt and pepper. Bind together with the beaten egg. Divide the stuffing between the pieces of meat and spread evenly almost to the edges. Roll up and secure with string. Heat the lard or margarine in the cooker, add the beef and brown evenly on all sides. Lift out and drain well. Drain off the excess lard or margarine from the cooker. Add the stock or water and stock cube and wine to the cooker and return to the heat. Stir well to remove any residues from the base of the cooker. Replace the beef roulades in the cooker with a little more salt and pepper. Close the cooker, bring to H pressure and cook for 25 minutes. Reduce the pressure quickly. Lift out the roulades to a warm serving dish, remove the string and keep hot.

Return the open cooker to the heat. Add the flour blended with a little cold water and stir constantly until the sauce boils and thickens, simmer for 1 minute. Taste and adjust the seasoning as necessary before pouring the sauce over the roulades. Sprinkle liberally with chopped parsley before serving.

Braised beef with peppers; Beef and bean casserole;
Above: Beef roulades

81

Beef and vegetable pie

Meat filling for pies will not take long to cook if you use a pressure cooker.

METRIC	IMPERIAL
50 g lard or margarine	2 oz lard or margarine
500 g stewing beef, trimmed and cubed	1 lb stewing beef, trimmed and cubed
1 onion, peeled and sliced	1 onion, peeled and sliced
2 carrots, scraped and sliced	2 carrots, scraped and sliced
300 ml brown stock or water and $\frac{1}{2}$ beef stock cube	$\frac{1}{2}$ pint brown stock or water and $\frac{1}{2}$ beef stock cube
salt	salt
freshly ground black pepper	freshly ground black pepper
2 × 15 ml spoons tomato purée	2 tablespoons tomato purée
1 × 100 g packet frozen peas	1 × 4 oz packet frozen peas
Pastry:	**Pastry:**
175 g flour	6 oz flour
pinch of salt	pinch of salt
40 g margarine	$1\frac{1}{2}$ oz margarine
40 g lard	$1\frac{1}{2}$ oz lard
2 × 15 ml spoons cold water	2 tablespoons cold water
a little milk	a little milk

Pie Filling: H Pressure – 15 minutes
Pie Crust: Oven – 200°C, 400°F or Gas Mark 6

METHOD

Heat the lard or margarine in the cooker. Sauté the beef and vegetables until the beef is browned and the vegetables are beginning to colour. Remove the cooker from the heat. Stir in the stock or water and stock cube, salt, pepper and tomato purée. Stir well to remove any residues from the base of the cooker. Close the cooker, bring to H pressure and cook for 15 minutes. Reduce the pressure quickly. Taste and adjust the seasoning as necessary.

While the meat is cooking make the pastry. Sift the flour and salt into a mixing bowl. Add the fats, cut into small pieces and rub into the flour until the mixture resembles fine breadcrumbs. Stir in sufficient water to form a firm dough that leaves the sides of the bowl cleanly. Turn on to a floured board and knead lightly. If possible wrap in foil or grease-proof paper and chill in the refrigerator for 15 to 30 minutes.

Transfer the meat mixture to a 900 ml /1$\frac{1}{2}$ pint pie dish and stir in the frozen peas. Roll out the pastry to fit the top of the pie dish. Cut a strip of pastry to go round the lip of the pie dish. Wet the lip and press on the strip of pastry. Wet the strip and cover with the pastry lid, sealing the edges well and making a steam hole in the centre of the pie crust. Decorate the top with leaves made from pastry trimmings. Brush with a little milk. Bake in a fairly hot oven for 25 minutes or until the pastry is golden brown.

Steak and mushroom pudding

A variation on an old-time favourite.

METRIC	IMPERIAL
500 g stewing beef, trimmed and cubed	1 lb stewing beef, trimmed and cubed
25 g flour	1 oz flour
salt	salt
freshly ground black pepper	freshly ground black pepper
1 small onion, peeled and chopped	1 small onion, peeled and chopped
100 g small button mushrooms, cleaned	4 oz small button mushrooms, cleaned
450 ml brown stock or water and $\frac{1}{2}$ beef stock cube	$\frac{3}{4}$ pint brown stock or water and $\frac{1}{2}$ beef stock cube
1 bay leaf	1 bay leaf
butter or margarine for greasing	butter or margarine for greasing
900 ml boiling water	1$\frac{1}{2}$ pints boiling water
a little lemon juice	a little lemon juice
Suet pastry:	**Suet pastry:**
225 g self-raising flour	8 oz self-raising flour
1 × 2.5 ml spoon salt	$\frac{1}{2}$ teaspoon salt
100 g shredded beef suet	4 oz shredded beef suet
150 ml cold water	$\frac{1}{4}$ pint cold water

Steak and mushroom pudding; Beef and vegetable pie

Meat filling: H Pressure – 15 minutes
Pudding: Steaming – 10 minutes
           L Pressure – 30 minutes OR
           H Pressure – 20 minutes

METHOD

Coat the meat in flour seasoned with salt and pepper. Put the meat, onion, mushrooms, stock or water and stock cube and bay leaf into the cooker. Close the cooker, bring to H pressure and cook for 15 minutes. Reduce the pressure quickly. Allow the meat to cool slightly and remove the bay leaf. Taste and adjust the seasoning as necessary.

Meanwhile make the suet pastry. Sift the flour and salt into a mixing bowl. Stir in the suet with sufficient cold water to form an elastic dough that leaves the sides of the bowl cleanly. Turn on to a floured board and knead lightly. Take two-thirds of the pastry and roll into a round large enough to line a 900 ml/1½ pint pudding basin. Grease the basin with a little butter or margarine and line with the pastry. Roll out the remaining pastry into a round large enough to form a lid for the pudding basin.

Put the meat mixture into the pastry-lined basin. Add sufficient gravy so that the basin is two-thirds full, reserve the remaining gravy to serve with the pudding. Wet the edges of the pastry lid, place over the meat and seal the edges well. Cover with a double layer of greased greaseproof paper or a single thickness of greased aluminium foil, pleated in the centre to allow for expansion. Tie down with string.

Have the water and a little lemon juice boiling in the cooker and add the trivet, rim side down. Stand the pudding on the trivet, close the cooker and steam gently, without the weights, for 10 minutes. Raise the heat, bring to L or H pressure and cook for 30 or 20 minutes accordingly. Reduce the pressure slowly. Taste and adjust the seasoning of the reserved gravy, thicken if liked and serve with the pudding.

Cheesy beef roll

METRIC	IMPERIAL
175 g self-raising flour	6 oz self-raising flour
1 × 2.5 ml spoon salt	½ teaspoon salt
50 g finely grated Cheddar cheese	2 oz finely grated Cheddar cheese
75 g shredded beef suet	3 oz shredded beef suet
approx. 150 ml cold water	approx. ¼ pint cold water
900 ml boiling water	1½ pints boiling water
little lemon juice	little lemon juice

Filling:

225 g minced beef	8 oz minced beef
1 small onion, peeled and finely chopped	1 small onion, peeled and finely chopped
1 × 15 ml spoon Worcestershire sauce	1 tablespoon Worcestershire sauce
salt	salt
freshly ground black pepper	freshly ground black pepper

**Steaming – 10 minutes
L Pressure – 30 minutes OR
H Pressure – 20 minutes**

METHOD

Sift the flour and salt into a mixing bowl. Add the cheese and suet and stir thoroughly. Gradually add sufficient water until a smooth, elastic dough is formed which leaves the sides of the bowl cleanly. Turn out on to a floured board and knead lightly. Roll into an oblong a little narrower than the base of the cooker and approximately 5 mm/¼ inch thick.

For the filling, mix together the beef, onion and Worcestershire sauce and add a little salt and pepper. Spread the filling evenly over the pastry, almost to the edges. Wet the edges with a little water and roll up swiss-roll style, sealing the edges well. Place the roll, seam-side down, on a double thickness of greased greaseproof paper or a greased piece of aluminium foil. Wrap loosely, making a pleat in the centre to allow for expansion and tie at the ends. Have the water and lemon juice boiling in the cooker and add the trivet, rim side down. Place the roll on to the trivet. Close the cooker and steam, without the weights, for 10 minutes. Raise the heat, bring to L or H pressure and cook for 30 or 20 minutes accordingly. Reduce the pressure slowly. Serve with fresh green vegetables.

Cheesy beef roll; Orange lamb shoulder; Navarin of lamb

Orange lamb shoulder

METRIC	IMPERIAL
1.5 kg boned shoulder of lamb	3 lb boned shoulder of lamb
salt	salt
freshly ground black pepper	freshly ground black pepper
75 g fresh white breadcrumbs	3 oz fresh white breadcrumbs
75 g mushrooms, cleaned and chopped	3 oz mushrooms, cleaned and chopped
50 g sultanas	2 oz sultanas
1 small onion, peeled and grated	1 small onion, peeled and grated
1 × 2.5 ml spoon dried marjoram	½ teaspoon dried marjoram
finely grated rind of 2 oranges	finely grated rind of 2 oranges
1 egg, beaten	1 egg, beaten
25 g lard or margarine	1 oz lard or margarine
750 ml hot brown stock or water and ½ beef stock cube	1½ pints hot brown stock or water and ½ beef stock cube

To finish:

2 × 15 ml spoons redcurrant jelly	2 tablespoons redcurrant jelly
2 × 5 ml spoons cornflour	2 teaspoons cornflour
little water	little water

H Pressure – 55 minutes

METHOD

Trim the lamb of any excess fat. Lay the lamb, skin side down, and season the upper surface with salt and pepper. Mix together the breadcrumbs, mushrooms, sultanas, onion, marjoram, orange rind and a little salt and pepper. Bind together with the egg. Spread the stuffing over the surface of the meat to within 2.5 cm/1 inch of the edges. Roll up as tightly as possible and secure at intervals with string. Heat the lard or margarine in the cooker and brown the lamb evenly all over. Lift out and drain off the excess lard or margarine from the cooker. Add the hot stock or water and stock cube to the cooker, stir well to remove any residues from the base of the cooker. Put the trivet into the cooker, rim side down and place the lamb on the trivet. Close the cooker, bring to H pressure and cook for 55 minutes. Reduce the pressure quickly. Lift out the joint to a warm serving dish, remove the string and keep hot. Remove the trivet from the cooker. Return the open cooker to the heat, stir in the redcurrant jelly and the cornflour blended with a little water. Simmer and stir constantly until the sauce is thickened. Taste and adjust the seasoning and serve with the lamb.

Navarin of lamb

METRIC	IMPERIAL
25 g lard or margarine	1 oz lard or margarine
1 large onion, peeled and sliced	1 large onion, peeled and sliced
1 garlic clove, crushed	1 garlic clove, crushed
2 breasts of lamb, chopped into single rib pieces	2 breasts of lamb, chopped into single rib pieces
25 g flour	1 oz flour
salt	salt
freshly ground black pepper	freshly ground black pepper
1 × 400 g can tomatoes	1 × 14 oz can tomatoes
300 ml white stock or water and ½ chicken stock cube	½ pint white stock or water and ½ chicken stock cube
225 g carrots, scraped and sliced	8 oz carrots, scraped and sliced
1 × 5 ml spoon mixed herbs	1 teaspoon mixed herbs

To finish:

1 × 15 ml spoon flour	1 tablespoon flour
little water	little water
a little freshly chopped parsley	a little freshly chopped parsley

H Pressure – 12 minutes

METHOD

Heat the lard or margarine in the cooker. Sauté the onion and garlic until both are beginning to colour. Lift out and drain well. Coat the meat pieces in the flour, seasoned with salt and pepper and fry until evenly browned all over. Lift out and drain well. Drain off any excess lard or margarine from the cooker. Return the cooker to the heat and stir in the tomatoes, stock or water and stock cube, carrots and herbs. Stir well to remove any residues from the base of the cooker. Return the meat, onion and garlic to the cooker. Close the cooker, bring to H pressure and cook for 12 minutes. Reduce the pressure quickly. Skim off any excess fat. Blend the flour with a little water. Return the open cooker to the heat and stir in the blended flour. Cook until thickened, stirring constantly. Taste and adjust the seasoning as necessary. Garnish with a little chopped parsley.

Lamb Italian

METRIC	IMPERIAL
8 lamb cutlets	8 lamb cutlets
25 g lard or margarine	1 oz lard or margarine
8 small onions, peeled	8 small onions, peeled
1 × 225 g can tomatoes	1 × 8 oz can tomatoes
1 garlic clove, crushed	1 garlic clove, crushed
50 g mushrooms, washed and thickly sliced	2 oz mushrooms, washed and thickly sliced
150 ml water	¼ pint water
1 × 5 ml spoon dried oregano	1 teaspoon dried oregano
salt	salt
freshly ground black pepper	freshly ground black pepper
2 × 5 ml spoons cornflour	2 teaspoons cornflour
little water	little water

H Pressure – 8 minutes

METHOD

Trim all but a thin layer of fat from the cutlets. Heat the lard or margarine in the cooker. Fry the cutlets and onions until the cutlets are brown on both sides. Remove both from the cooker and drain well. Pour off the remaining lard or margarine from the cooker. Return the cooker to the heat and add the tomatoes, garlic, mushrooms, water and oregano. Stir well to remove any residues from the base of the cooker. Return the cutlets and onions to the cooker with a little salt and pepper. Close the cooker, bring to H pressure and cook for 8 minutes. Reduce the pressure quickly. Lift out the cutlets and vegetables to a warm dish and keep hot. Return the cooker to the heat and stir in the cornflour blended with a little water. Bring to the boil stirring constantly. Taste and adjust the seasoning as necessary before pouring the sauce over the cutlets.

Lamb hot-pot

METRIC	IMPERIAL
100 g small haricot beans	4 oz small haricot beans
boiling water	boiling water
50 g lard or margarine	2 oz lard or margarine
1 kg middle or scrag neck of lamb, chopped and trimmed	2 lb middle or scrag neck of lamb, chopped and trimmed
1 large onion, peeled and sliced	1 large onion, peeled and sliced
1 turnip or parsnip, peeled and cubed	1 turnip or parsnip, peeled and cubed
2 large carrots, peeled and sliced	2 large carrots, peeled and sliced
750 ml hot brown stock or water and ½ beef stock cube	1¼ pints hot brown stock or water and ½ beef stock cube
salt	salt
freshly ground black pepper	freshly ground black pepper
1 bay leaf	1 bay leaf
1 × 15 ml spoon cornflour	1 tablespoon cornflour
a little cold water	a little cold water
finely chopped parsley, to garnish	finely chopped parsley, to garnish

Lamb Italian

H Pressure – 15 minutes

METHOD

Place the beans in a basin. Cover with boiling water and leave to soak for 1 hour. Heat the lard or margarine in the cooker and brown the meat evenly on both sides. Lift out and drain well. Fry the vegetables until they are beginning to colour. Remove the cooker from the heat and carefully drain off any excess lard or margarine. Add the stock or water and stock cube, salt, pepper and bay leaf to the cooker. Stir well to remove any residues from the base of the cooker. Return the meat and drained beans to the cooker. Close the cooker, bring to H pressure and cook for 15 minutes. Reduce the pressure slowly and remove the bay leaf. Blend the cornflour with a little water. Return the open cooker to the heat and add the blended cornflour. Cook, stirring constantly, until thickened. Taste and adjust the seasoning as necessary and serve garnished with chopped parsley.

Lemon and mushroom breast of lamb

METRIC

50 g fresh white breadcrumbs
1 × 5 ml spoon finely grated
  lemon rind
2 × 15 ml spoons lemon juice
50 g mushrooms, cleaned and
  chopped
1 small onion, peeled and
  finely chopped
1 × 2.5 ml spoon dried
  rosemary
salt
freshly ground black pepper
1 egg, beaten
1 kg breast of lamb, trimmed
  and boned
25 g lard or margarine
450 ml hot brown stock or
  water and ½ beef stock cube

IMPERIAL

2 oz fresh white breadcrumbs
1 teaspoon finely grated
  lemon rind
2 tablespoons lemon juice
2 oz mushrooms, cleaned and
  chopped
1 small onion, peeled and
  finely chopped
½ teaspoon dried rosemary
salt
freshly ground black pepper
1 egg, beaten
2 lb breast of lamb, trimmed
  and boned
1 oz lard or margarine
¾ pint hot brown stock or
  water and ½ beef stock cube

H Pressure – 30 minutes

METHOD

Mix together the breadcrumbs, lemon rind and juice, mushrooms, onion, rosemary and salt and pepper. Bind with the egg. Lay the lamb, skin side down, and spread the stuffing over the lamb to within 2.5 cm/1 inch of the edges. Roll up and tie securely at intervals with string. Heat the lard or margarine in the cooker and brown the lamb well on all sides. Lift out and drain off any excess lard or margarine from the cooker. Add the hot stock or water and stock cube and stir well to remove any residues from the base of the cooker. Put the trivet in the cooker, rim side down. Stand the joint on the trivet and season well with salt and pepper. Close the cooker, bring to H pressure and cook for 30 minutes. Reduce the pressure quickly. Remove the string from the meat before serving.

Lamb hot-pot; Lemon and mushroom breast of lamb

Lamb bourguignon

METRIC

2 × 15 ml spoons cooking oil
225 g small pickling onions,
  peeled
1 garlic clove, crushed
750 g lamb from shoulder or
  leg, cubed
100 g unsmoked streaky
  bacon, rinded and chopped
100 g button mushrooms,
  cleaned
2 × 15 ml spoons tomato
  purée
450 ml red wine
  (Burgundy-type)
salt
freshly ground black pepper

IMPERIAL

2 tablespoons cooking oil
8 oz small pickling onions,
  peeled
1 garlic clove, crushed
1½ lb lamb from shoulder or
  leg, cubed
4 oz unsmoked streaky
  bacon, rinded and chopped
4 oz button mushrooms,
  cleaned
2 tablespoons tomato purée
¾ pint red wine
  (Burgundy-type)
salt
freshly ground black pepper

To finish:

1 × 15 ml spoon flour
little water
a little freshly chopped
  parsley

To finish:

1 tablespoon flour
little water
a little freshly chopped
  parsley

H Pressure – 12 minutes

METHOD

Heat the oil in the cooker. Sauté the onions and garlic until they are beginning to colour. Add the meat and bacon and fry until the meat is evenly browned. Add the mushrooms, tomato purée, wine and a little salt and pepper. Stir well to remove any residues from the base of the cooker and bring to the boil. Close the cooker, bring to H pressure and cook for 12 minutes. Reduce the pressure quickly. Blend the flour with a little water. Return the open cooker to the heat. Stir in the blended flour and cook until thickened, stirring constantly. Taste and adjust the seasoning as necessary. Garnish with a little chopped parsley.

Pork spareribs in cider

METRIC	IMPERIAL
2 × 15 ml spoons cooking oil	2 tablespoons cooking oil
4 pork sparerib chops, trimmed	4 pork sparerib chops, trimmed
1 onion, peeled and chopped	1 onion, peeled and chopped
2 stalks celery, scrubbed and chopped	2 stalks celery, scrubbed and chopped
450 ml dry cider	¾ pint dry cider
salt	salt
freshly ground black pepper	freshly ground black pepper
1 × 2.5 ml spoon dried sage	½ teaspoon dried sage
2 × 5 ml spoons cornflour	2 teaspoons cornflour
little water	little water

H Pressure – 10 minutes

METHOD

Heat the oil in the cooker and brown the chops well on both sides. Add the onion and celery and cook until both are beginning to colour. Remove the chops and vegetables from the cooker and drain off any excess oil from the cooker. Away from the heat add the cider to the cooker. Stir to remove any residues from the base of the cooker. Return the chops and vegetables to the cooker with a little salt, pepper and the sage. Close the cooker, bring to H pressure and cook for 10 minutes. Reduce the pressure quickly. Lift out the chops to a warm dish and keep hot. Return the open cooker to the heat. Add the cornflour blended with a little cold water and stir constantly. Bring to the boil and simmer for 1 minute. Taste and adjust the seasoning as necessary before serving the sauce with the chops.

Lamb bourguignon; Pork spareribs in cider;
Pork chops with herbs

Pork chops with herbs

If the fresh herbs are out of season or difficult to obtain substitute dried herbs, but use half the quantity given for the fresh herbs.

METRIC	IMPERIAL
25 g lard or margarine	1 oz lard or margarine
4 pork chops	4 pork chops
450 ml hot brown stock or water and ½ beef stock cube	¾ pint hot brown stock or water and ½ beef stock cube
1 onion, peeled and chopped	1 onion, peeled and chopped
1 × 2.5 ml spoon chopped fresh sage	½ teaspoon chopped fresh sage
1 × 2.5 ml spoon chopped fresh thyme	½ teaspoon chopped fresh thyme
1 × 5 ml spoon chopped fresh parsley	1 teaspoon chopped fresh parsley
salt	salt
freshly ground black pepper	freshly ground black pepper
2 × 5 ml spoons flour	2 teaspoons flour
little water	little water

H Pressure – 10 minutes

METHOD

Heat the lard or margarine in the cooker and brown the chops on both sides. Lift the chops out and drain off the excess lard or margarine from the cooker. Add the stock or water and stock cube to the cooker and stir well to remove any residues from the base of the cooker. Place the trivet, rim side down, in the cooker. Place the chops on the trivet and carefully sprinkle each with a mixture of the onion, herbs, salt and pepper. Close the cooker, bring to H pressure and cook for 10 minutes. Reduce the pressure quickly. Carefully lift out the chops with herb topping to a warm dish and keep hot. Return the open cooker to the heat and add the flour blended with a little water. Cook, stirring continuously, until boiling and thickened. Taste and adjust the seasoning as necessary. Serve the sauce around the chops.

Paprika pork

METRIC	IMPERIAL
750 g boned pork shoulder, trimmed and cubed	1½ lb boned pork shoulder, trimmed and cubed
seasoned flour	seasoned flour
50 g butter or oil	2 oz butter or oil
2 garlic cloves, crushed	2 garlic cloves, crushed
3 × 5 ml spoons paprika pepper	3 teaspoons paprika pepper
300 ml white stock or water and ½ chicken stock cube	½ pint white stock or water and ½ chicken stock cube
150 ml dry sherry	¼ pint dry sherry
100 g mushrooms, cleaned and thickly sliced	4 oz mushrooms, cleaned and thickly sliced
1 bay leaf	1 bay leaf
salt	salt
150 ml fresh single cream	¼ pint fresh single cream

H Pressure – 15 minutes

METHOD

Coat the pork pieces in seasoned flour and shake off any excess flour. Heat the butter or oil in the cooker and sauté the pork pieces until evenly browned. Lift the pork out and drain well. Stir the garlic and paprika pepper into the cooking juices. Away from the heat add the stock or water and stock cube and sherry and stir well to remove any residues from the base of the cooker. Return the pork to the cooker with the mushrooms, bay leaf and a little salt. Close the cooker, bring to H pressure and cook for 15 minutes. Reduce the pressure quickly and remove the bay leaf. Taste and adjust the seasoning as necessary and stir the cream into the sauce just before serving. Do not reheat after the cream has been added. Serve with plain rice or buttered noodles.

Piquant pork casserole

METRIC	IMPERIAL
4 × 15 ml spoons cooking oil	4 tablespoons cooking oil
1 large onion, peeled and roughly chopped	1 large onion, peeled and roughly chopped
1 garlic clove, crushed	1 garlic clove, crushed
750 g pork shoulder, trimmed and cubed	1½ lb pork shoulder, trimmed and cubed
1 × 298 g can condensed consommé	1 × 10½ oz can condensed consommé
150 ml brown stock or water and ½ beef stock cube	¼ pint brown stock or water and ½ beef stock cube
2 × 15 ml spoons tomato purée	2 tablespoons tomato purée
1 × 15 ml spoon brown sugar	1 tablespoon brown sugar
1 × 15 ml spoon malt vinegar	1 tablespoon malt vinegar
1 red pepper, cored, seeded and sliced	1 red pepper, cored, seeded and sliced
1 × 5 ml spoon caraway seeds	1 teaspoon caraway seeds
salt	salt
freshly ground black pepper	freshly ground black pepper
1 × 15 ml spoon cornflour	1 tablespoon cornflour
little water	little water

Paprika pork

H Pressure – 15 minutes

METHOD

Heat the oil in the cooker. Add the onion and garlic and sauté until both are beginning to colour. Lift out and drain well. Add the pork to the hot oil and brown quickly and evenly. Lift out the pork and drain off any excess oil from the cooker. Away from the heat add the consommé, stock or water and stock cube and tomato purée to the cooker. Stir well to remove any residues from the base of the cooker. Return the cooker to the heat with the meat, onion, garlic, brown sugar, vinegar, red pepper and caraway seeds. Stir well and add a little salt and pepper. Close the cooker, bring to H pressure and cook for 15 minutes. Reduce the pressure quickly. Blend the cornflour with a little cold water. Return the open cooker to the heat. Add the cornflour and stir constantly until the sauce is boiling and thickened. Simmer for 1 minute. Taste and adjust the seasoning as necessary before serving.

Apricot stuffed tenderloins

Apricot stuffed tenderloins; Piquant pork casserole

METRIC
*2 medium pork tenderloins,
  approx. 500 g each*
50 g fresh white breadcrumbs
*1 × 15 ml spoon chopped
  fresh sage*
*1 small onion, peeled and
  grated*
*1 × 422 g can apricots,
  drained*
salt
freshly ground black pepper
4 × 15 ml spoons cooking oil
*300 ml hot white stock or
  water and ½ chicken stock
  cube*
300 ml dry white wine
*beurre manié made with
  25 g butter mixed with
  1 × 15 ml spoon flour*

To finish:
*small bunch of watercress,
  washed and trimmed*

IMPERIAL
*2 medium pork tenderloins,
  approx. 1 lb each*
2 oz fresh white breadcrumbs
*1 tablespoon chopped fresh
  sage*
*1 small onion, peeled and
  grated*
*1 × 15 oz can apricots,
  drained*
salt
freshly ground black pepper
4 tablespoons cooking oil
*½ pint hot white stock or
  water and ½ chicken stock
  cube*
½ pint dry white wine
*beurre manié made with
  1 oz butter, mixed with
  1 tablespoon flour*

To finish:
*small bunch of watercress,
  washed and trimmed*

H Pressure – 20 minutes

METHOD
Carefully slice each tenderloin almost through lengthways, open out and flatten slightly by beating with a rolling pin. Mix together the breadcrumbs, sage and onion. Chop all but 8 of the apricots and reserve these for garnish. Add the chopped apricots to the stuffing and season lightly with salt and pepper. Spread the stuffing along the centre of each tenderloin, fold over and secure with string at close intervals. Heat the oil in the cooker and brown the meat carefully on all sides. Lift the meat out and drain off the excess oil from the cooker. Add the stock or water and stock cube and wine to the cooker. Return to the heat and stir well to remove any residues from the base of the cooker. Replace the meat and season lightly with salt and pepper. Close the cooker, bring to H pressure and cook for 20 minutes. Reduce the pressure quickly. Lift out the meat, remove the string and place on a warm dish, keep hot. Return the open cooker to the heat, add the beurre manié in small pieces, stirring constantly. Cook until the sauce is thickened. Taste and adjust the seasoning before serving the sauce around the meat. Garnish with reserved apricot halves and bunches of watercress.

91

Pork and cheese escalopes ; Pork with prune stuffing

Pork and cheese escalopes

METRIC

75 g fresh white breadcrumbs
50 g Cheddar cheese, finely
  grated
25 g shredded beef suet
1 × 5 ml spoon dried sage
salt
freshly ground black pepper
1 egg, beaten
4 pork escalopes (approx.
  100 g each), beaten
25 g butter or oil
450 ml white stock or water
  and ½ chicken stock cube
Sauce:
25 g butter or margarine
25 g flour
a little milk
75 g Cheddar cheese, finely
  grated

IMPERIAL

3 oz fresh white breadcrumbs
2 oz Cheddar cheese, finely
  grated
1 oz shredded beef suet
1 teaspoon dried sage
salt
freshly ground black pepper
1 egg, beaten
4 pork escalopes (approx.
  4 oz each), beaten
1 oz butter or oil
¾ pint white stock or water
  and ½ chicken stock cube
Sauce:
1 oz butter or margarine
1 oz flour
a little milk
3 oz Cheddar cheese, finely
  grated

H Pressure – 12 minutes

METHOD

For the stuffing, mix together the breadcrumbs, cheese, suet, sage and salt and pepper. Bind with the beaten egg. Divide the stuffing between the escalopes and spread to the edges. Roll up the escalopes and secure with string. Heat the butter or oil in the cooker, add the escalopes and brown quickly on all sides. Lift out and drain well. Drain off excess butter or oil from the cooker. Pour in the stock or water and stock cube and return to the heat. Stir well to remove any residues from the base of the cooker. Return the escalopes to the cooker with a little salt and pepper. Close the cooker, bring to H pressure and cook for 12 minutes. Reduce the pressure quickly. Lift out the escalopes to a warmed serving dish and keep hot, remove the string. Strain the cooking liquid and make up to 450 ml/¾ pint with the milk from the sauce.

Melt the butter or margarine in the rinsed and dried cooker, add the flour and cook for 1 to 2 minutes. Remove from the heat and stir in the liquid gradually. Return to the heat and bring to the boil. Stir constantly and simmer for 1 minute. Remove from the heat, stir in the cheese, taste and adjust the seasoning as necessary before pouring the sauce over the pork escalopes.

Pork with prune stuffing

METRIC	IMPERIAL
100 g prunes	4 oz prunes
cold water	cold water
75 g fresh white breadcrumbs	3 oz fresh white breadcrumbs
finely grated rind of 1 lemon	finely grated rind of 1 lemon
salt	salt
freshly ground black pepper	freshly ground black pepper
1 egg, beaten	1 egg, beaten
1.5 kg blade bone joint of pork, boned and rinded	3 lb blade bone joint of pork, boned and rinded
50 g lard or margarine	2 oz lard or margarine
600 ml hot brown stock or water and ½ beef stock cube	1 pint hot brown stock or water and ½ beef stock cube
2 × 5 ml spoons cornflour	2 teaspoons cornflour
little water	little water
small bunch watercress, to garnish	small bunch watercress, to garnish

H Pressure – 15 minutes per 500 g/1 lb stuffed weight

METHOD

Soak the prunes in cold water for several hours or overnight. Drain and dry well, remove the stones and chop. Mix the prunes with the breadcrumbs, lemon rind and a little salt and pepper. Bind with sufficient egg to make a firm stuffing. Make a deep slit in the flesh side of the pork and pack the stuffing into the slit. Make the joint into a roll and secure at intervals with string. Sprinkle well with salt and pepper.

Heat the lard or margarine in the cooker and brown the joint evenly all over. Lift out and drain off any excess lard or margarine from the cooker. Add the stock or water and stock cube and the trivet, rim side down. Stand the joint on the trivet. Close the cooker, bring to H pressure and cook for the calculated time. Reduce the pressure quickly. Lift out the joint, remove the string and place on a warmed dish, keep hot. Mix the cornflour with a little water and add to the cooker. Cook over a gentle heat, stirring constantly, until the sauce thickens. Taste and adjust the seasoning as necessary and serve with the pork. Garnish with watercress.

Hungarian veal chops

METRIC	IMPERIAL
4 veal loin chops (approx. 750 g–1 kg)	4 veal loin chops (approx. 1½–2 lb)
25 g flour	1 oz flour
salt	salt
freshly ground black pepper	freshly ground black pepper
25 g butter	1 oz butter
1 onion, peeled and sliced	1 onion, peeled and sliced
175 g large mushrooms, cleaned and sliced	6 oz large mushrooms, cleaned and sliced
3 × 5 ml spoons paprika pepper	3 teaspoons paprika pepper
1 × 63 g can tomato purée	1 × 2¼ oz can tomato purée
450 ml white stock or water and ½ chicken stock cube	¾ pint white stock or water and ½ chicken stock cube

To finish:
150 ml carton soured cream
a little freshly chopped
  parsley

To finish:
¼ pint carton soured cream
a little freshly chopped
  parsley

H Pressure – 8 minutes

METHOD

Coat the chops in the flour seasoned with salt and pepper. Heat the butter in the cooker. Brown the chops on both sides, lift out and drain well. Sauté the onion and mushrooms until the onion begins to soften. Stir in the paprika pepper, tomato purée and stock or water and stock cube and cook for a few moments. Stir well to remove any residues from the base of the cooker. Return the chops to the cooker and bring to the boil. Close the cooker, bring to H pressure and cook for 8 minutes. Reduce the pressure quickly. Lift out the chops to a warm serving dish and keep hot. Stir the soured cream into the sauce or drizzle over after. Taste and adjust the seasoning as necessary before pouring the sauce over the chops. Garnish with a little chopped parsley.

Hungarian veal chops

Osso buco

This version of the classic Italian dish is cooked in minutes. The garnish is traditional.

METRIC	IMPERIAL
50 g butter	2 oz butter
1 large onion, peeled and coarsely chopped	1 large onion, peeled and coarsely chopped
1 garlic clove, crushed	1 garlic clove, crushed
2 small carrots, scraped and sliced	2 small carrots, scraped and sliced
1 kg shin of veal, cut into 5 cm pieces	2 lb shin of veal, cut into 2 inch pieces
300 ml hot white stock or water and ½ chicken stock cube	½ pint hot white stock or water and ½ chicken stock cube
150 ml dry white wine	¼ pint dry white wine
1 × 225 g can tomatoes, roughly chopped	1 × 8 oz can tomatoes, roughly chopped
2 × 15 ml spoons tomato purée	2 tablespoons tomato purée
1 × 2.5 ml spoon dried rosemary	½ teaspoon dried rosemary
salt	salt
freshly ground black pepper	freshly ground black pepper
2 × 5 ml spoons cornflour	2 teaspoons cornflour
little cold water	little cold water
Garnish:	**Garnish:**
2 × 15 ml spoons freshly chopped parsley	2 tablespoons freshly chopped parsley
1 garlic clove, crushed	1 garlic clove, crushed
finely grated rind of 1 lemon	finely grated rind of 1 lemon

H Pressure – 15 minutes

METHOD

Heat the butter in the cooker and sauté the onion, garlic and carrots until they are beginning to colour. Lift the vegetable mixture out of the cooker and drain well. Brown the pieces of veal, lift out and drain off the excess butter from the cooker. Add the stock or water and stock cube, wine, tomatoes, tomato purée, rosemary and a little salt and pepper to the cooker. Stir in the vegetables. Lastly, replace the meat pieces, standing them upright in the sauce. Close the cooker, bring to H pressure and cook for 15 minutes. Reduce the pressure quickly. While the veal is cooking mix together the ingredients for the garnish.

Transfer the veal to a hot serving dish. Add the cornflour, blended with a little cold water, to the sauce and cook, stirring constantly until boiling and thickened. Taste and adjust the seasoning as necessary, pour the sauce over the veal and sprinkle with the garnish. Serve with plain boiled rice or buttered noodles and a crisp green salad.

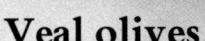

Veal olives

METRIC	IMPERIAL
4 veal escalopes, approx. 100 g each	4 veal escalopes, approx. 4 oz each
75 g fresh white breadcrumbs	3 oz fresh white breadcrumbs
1 × 5 ml spoon finely grated lemon rind	1 teaspoon finely grated lemon rind
1 × 15 ml spoon lemon juice	1 tablespoon lemon juice
1 × 2.5 ml spoon dried thyme	½ teaspoon dried thyme
1 × 2.5 ml spoon dried basil	½ teaspoon dried basil
50 g butter, melted	2 oz butter, melted
salt	salt
freshly ground black pepper	freshly ground black pepper
2 × 15 ml spoons cooking oil	2 tablespoons cooking oil
450 ml white stock or water and ½ chicken stock cube	¾ pint white stock or water and ½ chicken stock cube
1 × 15 ml spoon cornflour	1 tablespoon cornflour
little water	little water
150 ml single cream	¼ pint single cream
lemon wedges to garnish	lemon wedges to garnish

Osso buco; Veal olives; Veal and ham casserole

H Pressure – 10 minutes

METHOD

Beat the escalopes with a rolling pin until they are thin. Mix together the breadcrumbs, lemon rind and juice, herbs and melted butter and season lightly with salt and pepper. Divide the stuffing between the escalopes and spread almost to the edges of each. Roll the escalopes up and secure with string. Heat the oil in the cooker and brown the rolls evenly all over. Carefully drain off any excess oil from the cooker before adding the stock or water and stock cube. Close the cooker, bring to H pressure and cook for 10 minutes. Reduce the pressure quickly. Lift out the rolls, discard the string and keep hot. Return the open cooker to the heat. Stir in the cornflour blended with a little water and cook until boiling and thickened. Remove from the heat, stir in the cream and adjust the seasoning as necessary. Serve the sauce poured over the veal olives. Garnish with lemon wedges.

Veal and ham casserole

METRIC	IMPERIAL
25 g butter or margarine	1 oz butter or margarine
1 small onion, peeled and coarsely chopped	1 small onion, peeled and coarsely chopped
500–750 g stewing or pie veal, trimmed and cut into 2.5 cm cubes	1–1½ lb stewing or pie veal, trimmed and cut into 1 inch cubes
225 g ham steaks, cut into 2.5 cm squares	8 oz ham steaks, cut into 1 inch squares
600 ml hot white stock or water and ½ chicken stock cube	1 pint hot white stock or water and ½ chicken stock cube
100 g button mushrooms	4 oz button mushrooms
salt	salt
freshly ground black pepper	freshly ground black pepper
1 bay leaf	1 bay leaf
To finish:	**To finish:**
1 × 15 ml spoon cornflour	1 tablespoon cornflour
freshly chopped parsley	freshly chopped parsley

H Pressure – 10 minutes

METHOD

Heat the butter or margarine in the cooker and sauté the onion until just beginning to colour. Add the veal and ham, brown slightly and remove from the cooker. Drain off any excess butter or margarine from the cooker. Add the stock or water and stock cube to the cooker and return the meats and onion with the mushrooms. Add the salt, pepper and bay leaf. Close the cooker, bring to H pressure and cook for 10 minutes. Reduce the pressure quickly. Remove the bay leaf. Return the open cooker to the heat. Add the cornflour blended with a little cold water. Stir well until boiling and thickened. Taste and adjust the seasoning as necessary. Garnish liberally with chopped parsley.

Veal and asparagus casserole

A can of condensed soup is the basis of the sauce, therefore if liked, you can change the flavour of the soup to suit your taste. Celery or mushroom complement the delicate veal flavour.

METRIC	IMPERIAL
25 g butter or margarine	1 oz butter or margarine
1 small onion, peeled and chopped	1 small onion, peeled and chopped
750 g–1 kg stewing or pie veal, trimmed and cut into 2.5 cm cubes	1½–2 lb stewing or pie veal, trimmed and cut into 1 inch cubes
1 × 298 g can condensed asparagus soup	1 × 10½ oz can condensed asparagus soup
300 ml white stock or water	½ pint white stock or water
1 × 298 g can asparagus spears, drained	1 × 10½ oz can asparagus spears, drained
salt	salt
freshly ground black pepper	freshly ground black pepper
To finish:	**To finish:**
2 × 5 ml spoons cornflour	2 teaspoons cornflour
little water	little water
2 × 15 ml spoons single cream	2 tablespoons single cream

H Pressure – 10 minutes

METHOD

Heat the butter or margarine in the cooker and sauté the onion until just beginning to colour. Add the veal and brown lightly. Stir in the can of soup and white stock or water. Reserve 8 spears of asparagus for garnish and cut the rest into 2.5 cm/1 inch lengths. Add the asparagus to the cooker with a little salt and pepper and stir well. Close the cooker, bring to H pressure and cook for 10 minutes. Reduce the pressure quickly. Return the open cooker to the heat and add the cornflour blended with a little cold water. Stir until boiling and thickened. Taste and adjust the seasoning as necessary. Transfer the casserole to a serving dish. Garnish with the reserved asparagus spears and cream.

Bacon collar – Danish style

Any bacon joint may be used for this recipe but collar is a little more economical and slices well. See note on smoked joints, page 72.

METRIC	IMPERIAL
unsmoked collar joint of bacon up to 1.5 kg in weight	unsmoked collar joint of bacon up to 3 lb in weight
cold water	cold water
900 ml lager	1½ pints lager
1 small onion stuck with 6 cloves	1 small onion stuck with 6 cloves
1 bay leaf	1 bay leaf
a few black peppercorns	a few black peppercorns
a little chopped parsley to garnish	a little chopped parsley to garnish
Sauce:	**Sauce:**
25 g butter or margarine	1 oz butter or margarine
25 g flour	1 oz flour
150 ml milk	¼ pint milk
salt	salt
freshly ground black pepper	freshly ground black pepper

H Pressure – 12 minutes per 500 g/1 lb

METHOD

Put the bacon into the cooker and cover with cold water. Bring to the boil, remove from the heat and drain well. Place the trivet, rim side down, in the cooker and stand the bacon on the trivet. Add the lager, onion, bay leaf and peppercorns, which have been crushed in a paper bag with a rolling pin. Close the cooker, bring to H pressure and cook for the calculated time. Reduce the pressure quickly. Lift out the joint and allow to cool slightly before removing the skin. Keep hot. Drain off the cooking liquid, reserving 300 ml/½ pint for the sauce. Rinse and dry the cooker.

Melt the butter or margarine in the cooker, add the flour and cook for a few moments. Remove from the heat and add the milk and reserved cooking liquid, stirring well. Return to the heat and bring to the boil, stirring constantly. Simmer for 1 minute. Taste and adjust the seasoning as necessary. Slice the bacon thickly and arrange on a serving dish. Pour the sauce along the centre of the meat slices and garnish with a little chopped parsley. Serve with buttered new potatoes and a green vegetable.

To serve cold: allow the joint to cool in the cooking liquid. Strip off the skin and coat the fat with browned breadcrumbs. Serve with salad.

Bacon, leek and sage pudding

METRIC	IMPERIAL
200 g self-raising flour	*8 oz self-raising flour*
1 × 2.5 ml spoon salt	*½ teaspoon salt*
100 g shredded beef suet	*4 oz shredded beef suet*
150 ml cold water	*¼ pint cold water*
Filling:	**Filling:**
175 g unsmoked streaky	*6 oz unsmoked streaky*
* bacon rashers, rinded*	* bacon rashers, rinded*
1 leek, cleaned and thinly	*1 leek, cleaned and thinly*
* sliced*	* sliced*
1 × 5 ml spoon fresh sage or	*1 teaspoon fresh sage or*
* 1 × 2.5 ml spoon dried sage*	* ½ teaspoon dried sage*
salt	*salt*
freshly ground black pepper	*freshly ground black pepper*
900 ml boiling water	*1½ pints boiling water*
a little lemon juice	*a little lemon juice*

*Above: Bacon, leek and sage pudding; Bacon collar Danish style;
Veal and asparagus casserole*

**Steaming – 10 minutes
H Pressure – 20 minutes OR
L Pressure – 30 minutes**

METHOD

Sift the flour and salt into a mixing bowl. Stir in the suet and gradually add the water until a smooth elastic dough is formed, which leaves the sides of the bowl cleanly. Turn on to a floured board and knead lightly. Roll the pastry into an oblong a little narrower than the base of the cooker and approximately 5 mm/¼ inch thick. Put a layer of streaky bacon rashers over the pastry, slightly overlapping each rasher, to within 2.5 cm/1 inch of the edges. Cover evenly with the sliced leek, sage and a little salt and pepper. Brush the edges of the pastry with a little water and roll up, swiss-roll style, sealing all the edges well. Place the roll, seam-side down, on a greased double thickness of greaseproof paper or on a well-greased piece of aluminium foil. Wrap loosely, making a pleat in the centre to allow for expansion. Secure the greaseproof paper with string at the ends. Have the boiling water and a little lemon juice ready in the cooker. Add the trivet rim side down. Carefully stand the pudding on the trivet, close the cooker and steam gently, without the weights, for 10 minutes. Bring to H or L pressure and cook for 20 or 30 minutes accordingly. Reduce the pressure slowly. Serve sliced with a brown gravy and vegetables.

Barbecue glazed gammon

A 1.75–2 kg/3½–4 lb joint is the maximum size that the larger pressure cookers will take. Do ensure that there is sufficient room for a good circulation of steam, otherwise the joint will not cook evenly. See note on smoked joints, page 72.

METRIC
1.5 kg corner or middle gammon
cold water
1 × 411 g can peach halves, drained and juice reserved
1 bay leaf
a few black peppercorns
For the glaze:
3 × 15 ml spoons reserved peach juice
2 × 15 ml spoons demerara sugar
1 × 5 ml spoon mustard powder
1 × 5 ml spoon Worcestershire sauce
1 × 5 ml spoon tomato purée
1 × 5 ml spoon malt vinegar
a few cloves
a little demerara sugar for the peaches

IMPERIAL
3 lb corner or middle gammon
cold water
1 × 14½ oz can peach halves, drained and juice reserved
1 bay leaf
a few black peppercorns
For the glaze:
3 tablespoons reserved peach juice
2 tablespoons demerara sugar
1 teaspoon mustard powder
1 teaspoon Worcestershire sauce
1 teaspoon tomato purée
1 teaspoon malt vinegar
a few cloves
a little demerara sugar for the peaches

H Pressure – 8 minutes per 500 g/1 lb
Oven – 200°C, 400°F or Gas Mark 6 for 25 to 30 minutes

METHOD
Place the joint in the cooker, cover with cold water and bring to the boil. Remove the joint from the cooker and discard the liquid. Return the joint to the cooker and add the drained peach juice, reserving 3 × 15 ml spoons/3 tablespoons peach juice. Add sufficient water to cover the joint but make sure the cooker is not more than half full. Add the bay leaf and peppercorns, which have been crushed in a paper bag with a rolling pin. Close the cooker, bring to H pressure and cook for the calculated time. Reduce the pressure quickly. Lift out the joint and allow to cool slightly. Meanwhile, combine in a saucepan the reserved peach juice, demerara sugar, mustard powder, Worcestershire sauce, tomato purée and vinegar. Heat gently until the sugar is dissolved.

When the joint is cool enough to handle, strip the skin from the joint. Using a sharp knife, score the fat into a diamond pattern. Stand the joint in a roasting tin, brush liberally with the glaze and stud with the cloves. Bake in the oven for 15 minutes, then remove and pour over any remaining glaze. Put the peach halves around the joint and sprinkle with a little demerara sugar. Continue baking for a further 10 to 15 minutes. Serve hot in thick slices with parsleyed new potatoes and sweetcorn.

Bacon casserole with cider; Barbecue glazed gammon

Bacon casserole with cider

METRIC	IMPERIAL
100 g lentils	4 oz lentils
600 ml boiling water	1 pint boiling water
750 g unsmoked bacon collar or forehock, boned, trimmed and cut into 2.5 cm cubes	1½ lb unsmoked collar bacon or forehock, boned, trimmed and cut into 1 inch cubes
25 g butter or margarine	1 oz butter or margarine
1 large onion, peeled and sliced	1 large onion, peeled and sliced
3 stalks celery, scrubbed and coarsely chopped	3 stalks celery, scrubbed and coarsely chopped
2 small leeks, washed and cut into 2.5 cm pieces (reserve a little top leaf for garnish)	2 small leeks, washed and cut into 1 inch pieces (reserve a little top leaf for garnish)
300 ml dry cider	½ pint dry cider
300 ml white stock or water and ½ chicken stock cube	½ pint white stock or water and ½ chicken stock cube
freshly ground black pepper	freshly ground black pepper
pinch of dried sage	pinch of dried sage
1 × 15 ml spoon cornflour	1 tablespoon cornflour
little water	little water

H Pressure – 15 minutes

METHOD

Put the lentils in a basin, cover with water and soak for 1 hour. Place the bacon in the cooker with sufficient cold water to cover and bring to the boil. Discard water and put the bacon to one side. Rinse and dry the cooker. Heat the butter or margarine in the cooker and sauté the vegetables until they are beginning to colour. Add the bacon, drained lentils, cider, white stock or water and stock cube, pepper and sage and stir well. Close the cooker, bring to H pressure and cook for 15 minutes. Reduce the pressure slowly. Blend the cornflour with a little cold water and add to the cooker. Return the open cooker to the heat. Cook, stirring constantly, until the sauce is boiling and thickened. Taste and adjust the seasoning. Garnish with chopped leek tops.

Lamb's hearts with rosemary

METRIC	IMPERIAL
4 lamb's hearts	4 lamb's hearts
75 g fresh white breadcrumbs	3 oz fresh white breadcrumbs
1 small onion, peeled and finely chopped	1 small onion, peeled and finely chopped
2 rashers unsmoked streaky bacon, rinded and finely chopped	2 rashers unsmoked streaky bacon, rinded and finely chopped
1 × 5 ml spoon dried rosemary	1 teaspoon dried rosemary
1 egg, beaten	1 egg, beaten
salt	salt
freshly ground black pepper	freshly ground black pepper
25 g flour	1 oz flour
25 g lard or margarine	1 oz lard or margarine
600 ml hot brown stock or water and ½ beef stock cube	1 pint hot brown stock or water and ½ beef stock cube
1 × 15 ml spoon flour	1 tablespoon flour
little water	little water

Lamb's hearts with rosemary

H Pressure – 30 minutes

METHOD

Wash the hearts very thoroughly. Trim away any fat, tubes or gristle. Mix together the breadcrumbs, onion, bacon and rosemary, bind with the egg and season lightly with salt and pepper. Fill the hearts with the stuffing and close the opening with 2 large stitches made with strong thread. Coat the hearts in flour. Heat the lard or margarine in the cooker and brown the hearts evenly. Lift them out and drain off the excess lard or margarine from the cooker. Add the stock or water and stock cube to the cooker and return the hearts. Close the cooker, bring to H pressure and cook for 30 minutes. Reduce the pressure quickly. Lift out the hearts to a warmed dish, remove the thread and keep hot. Return the open cooker to the heat. Blend the flour with a little water and stir into the stock. Cook, stirring constantly, until the sauce is boiling and thickened. Taste and adjust the seasoning as necessary and pour the sauce around the hearts to serve.

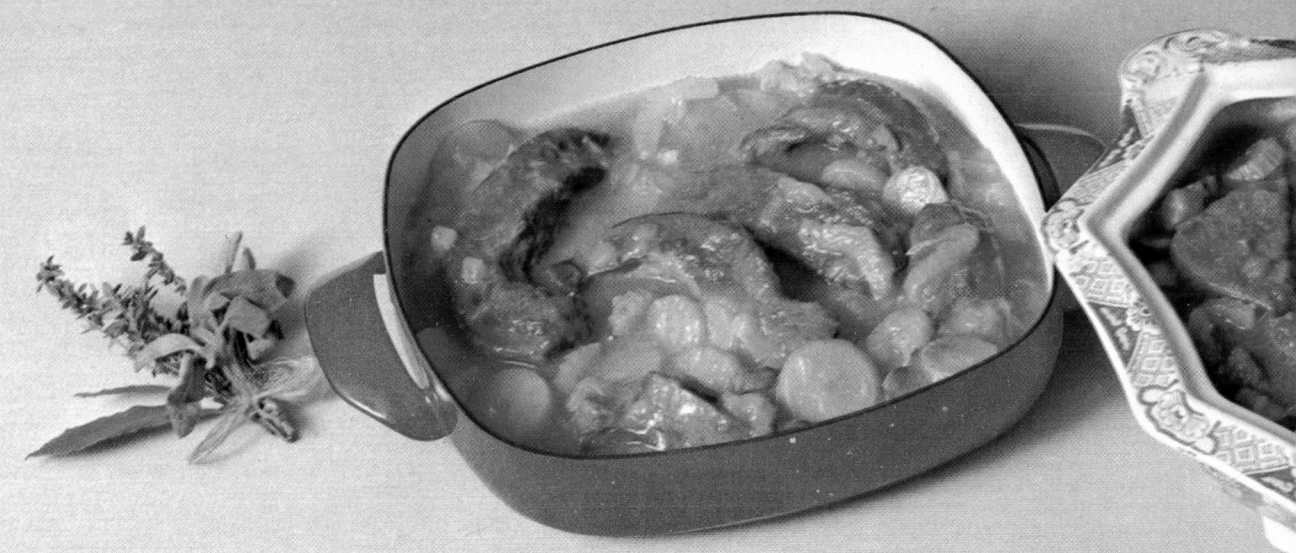

Braised ox heart

METRIC	IMPERIAL
750 g ox heart, cut into thick slices	1½ lb ox heart, cut into thick slices
50 g flour	2 oz flour
salt	salt
freshly ground black pepper	freshly ground black pepper
25 g lard or margarine	1 oz lard or margarine
1 large onion, peeled and sliced	1 large onion, peeled and sliced
2 celery stalks, scrubbed and chopped	2 celery stalks, scrubbed and chopped
2 large carrots, scraped and sliced	2 large carrots, scraped and sliced
600 ml hot brown stock or water and ½ beef stock cube	1 pint hot brown stock or water and ½ beef stock cube
2 × 15 ml spoons tomato purée	2 tablespoons tomato purée
bouquet garni	bouquet garni
1 × 15 ml spoon flour	1 tablespoon flour
little water	little water

H Pressure – 25 minutes

METHOD

Remove any tubes or fat from the heart. Coat in the flour seasoned with salt and pepper. Heat the lard or margarine in the cooker and brown the heart on both sides. Lift out and drain well. Fry the vegetables until they are beginning to colour. Lift the vegetables out and drain off the excess lard or margarine from the cooker. Add the stock or water and stock cube and tomato purée to the cooker. Stir to remove any residues from the base of the cooker. Return the vegetables together with the bouquet garni to the cooker and lay the slices of heart on the vegetables. Close the cooker, bring to H pressure and cook for 25 minutes. Reduce the pressure quickly. Lift out the heart to a warmed dish and keep hot. Discard the bouquet garni. Return the open cooker to the heat and stir in the flour blended with a little cold water. Stir constantly until the sauce is boiling and thickened. Taste and adjust the seasoning as necessary before serving the sauce around the heart.

Braised ox heart; Country liver casserole; Savoury liver with noodles

Country liver casserole

METRIC	IMPERIAL
50 g lard or margarine	2 oz lard or margarine
1 large onion, peeled and chopped	1 large onion, peeled and chopped
4 stalks celery, scrubbed and chopped	4 stalks celery, scrubbed and chopped
1 parsnip, peeled and diced	1 parsnip, peeled and diced
500–750 g pig's liver	1–1½ lb pig's liver
25 g flour	1 oz flour
salt	salt
freshly ground black pepper	freshly ground black pepper
450 ml hot brown stock or water and ½ beef stock cube	¾ pint hot brown stock or water and ½ beef stock cube
2 × 15 ml spoons tomato purée	2 tablespoons tomato purée
2 × 5 ml spoons chopped fresh parsley (optional)	2 teaspoons chopped fresh parsley (optional)

H Pressure – 6 minutes

METHOD

Heat the lard or margarine in the cooker. Fry the onion, celery and parsnip until they are beginning to colour. Lift out and drain well. Cut the liver into 1 cm/½ inch thick slices and coat in the flour seasoned with salt and pepper. Fry the liver quickly in the hot lard or margarine until lightly browned. Lift out and drain the excess lard or margarine from the cooker. Away from the heat, add the stock or water and stock cube and tomato purée to the cooker. Stir well to remove any residues from the base of the cooker. Return the vegetables and liver to the cooker with a little more salt and pepper. Close the cooker, bring to H pressure and cook for 6 minutes. Reduce the pressure quickly and taste and adjust the seasoning as necessary. Sprinkle with the chopped parsley before serving, if liked.

Savoury liver with noodles

METRIC
750 g pig's liver, cut into
  thin strips
25 g flour
salt
freshly ground black pepper
50 g lard or margarine
1 onion, peeled and chopped
1 × 400 g can tomatoes
600 ml hot brown stock or
  water and ½ beef stock cube
1 × 5 ml spoon dried oregano
75 g noodles

IMPERIAL
1½ lb pig's liver, cut into
  thin strips
1 oz flour
salt
freshly ground black pepper
2 oz lard or margarine
1 onion, peeled and chopped
1 × 14 oz can tomatoes
1 pint hot brown stock or
  water and ½ beef stock cube
1 teaspoon dried oregano
3 oz noodles

H Pressure – 5 minutes

METHOD
Coat the liver in the flour seasoned with salt and pepper.
Shake well to remove any surplus. Heat the lard or margarine in the cooker and sauté the liver and onion until
lightly browned. Lift out and drain well. Drain off the
excess lard or margarine from the cooker. Add the tomatoes
and stock or water and stock cube to the cooker and return
to the heat. Stir well to remove any residues from the base of
the cooker. Return the liver and onion to the cooker together with the oregano and noodles. Close the cooker,
bring to H pressure and cook for 5 minutes. Reduce the
pressure quickly. Taste and adjust the seasoning as necessary
and serve immediately garnished with parsley, if liked.

Chicken liver and brandy pâté

This pâté improves in flavour if it is made and stored in the refrigerator for a day or two before eating.

METRIC	IMPERIAL
225 g chicken livers	8 oz chicken livers
1 onion, peeled and chopped	1 onion, peeled and chopped
1 garlic clove, crushed	1 garlic clove, crushed
4 rashers unsmoked streaky bacon, rinded	4 rashers unsmoked streaky bacon, rinded
4 slices white bread (from a large loaf)	4 slices white bread (from a large loaf)
1 × 2.5 ml spoon dried mixed herbs	½ teaspoon dried mixed herbs
salt	salt
freshly ground black pepper	freshly ground black pepper
1 egg, beaten	1 egg, beaten
2 × 15 ml spoons brandy	2 tablespoons brandy
1 bay leaf	1 bay leaf
600 ml water	1 pint water
lemon juice	lemon juice

H Pressure – 20 minutes

METHOD

Put the livers, onion, garlic, bacon and bread through a mincer, using a fine cutter. Add the herbs, salt, pepper, egg and brandy and stir lightly to combine. Place pâté mixture in a lightly greased 600 ml/1 pint ovenproof dish and press the bay leaf lightly into the top. Cover with a double layer of greased greaseproof paper. Put the water, lemon juice and trivet into the cooker. Stand the dish on the trivet. Close the cooker, bring to H pressure and cook for 20 minutes. Reduce the pressure quickly. Remove the greaseproof paper from the pâté and cool thoroughly.

Farmer's kitchen pâté

Sage, liver and onion

METRIC	IMPERIAL
1 × 15 ml spoon cooking oil	1 tablespoon cooking oil
15 g butter	½ oz butter
1 onion, peeled and sliced	1 onion, peeled and sliced
25 g flour	1 oz flour
1 × 5 ml spoon dried sage	1 teaspoon dried sage
salt	salt
freshly ground black pepper	freshly ground black pepper
500 g pig's liver, sliced	1 lb pig's liver, sliced
450 ml hot brown stock or water and ½ beef stock cube	¾ pint hot brown stock or water and ½ beef stock cube
little water	little water

H Pressure – 6 minutes

METHOD

Heat the oil and butter in the cooker. Add the onion and fry until a light golden brown. Lift out the onion and drain well. Mix together the flour and sage with a little salt and pepper. Evenly coat the liver with the seasoned flour and reserve any leftover flour. Lightly brown the liver on both sides. Remove the cooker from the heat and take out the liver. Add the stock or water and stock cube and stir well to remove any residues from the base of the cooker. Return the liver and onion to the cooker. Close the cooker, bring to H pressure and cook for 6 minutes. Reduce the pressure quickly. Transfer the liver and onion to a warm dish and keep hot. Return the open cooker to the heat and stir in the reserved seasoned flour blended with a little water. Stir until thickened and taste and adjust the seasoning as necessary. Pour the sauce over the liver and serve immediately.

Farmer's kitchen pâté

METRIC

1 small onion, peeled
100 g belly of pork
100 g lean veal
225 g pig's liver
225 g unsmoked streaky
  bacon, rinded
salt
freshly ground black pepper
1 × 2.5 ml spoon dried thyme
1 × 1.25 ml spoon ground mace
4 × 15 ml spoons dry white
  wine
600 ml water
lemon juice

IMPERIAL

1 small onion, peeled
4 oz belly of pork
4 oz lean veal
8 oz pig's liver
8 oz unsmoked streaky
  bacon, rinded
salt
freshly ground black pepper
½ teaspoon dried thyme
¼ teaspoon ground mace
4 tablespoons dry white wine
1 pint water
lemon juice

H Pressure – 25 minutes

METHOD

Put the onion, pork, veal and liver through a mincer, using a fine cutter. Finely chop half the bacon and add to the minced meats. Add a little salt and pepper and the herbs to the meats. Bind with the white wine so the meat mixture has a soft consistency. Line a 500 g/1 lb loaf tin with the remaining rashers of streaky bacon. Fill with the pâté mixture and press down lightly. Cover with a double layer of greased greaseproof paper. Put the water, lemon juice and trivet into the cooker. Stand the loaf tin on the trivet. Close the cooker, bring to H pressure and cook for 25 minutes. Reduce the pressure quickly. Remove the pâté from the cooker. Remove the greaseproof paper, cover with a fresh piece of paper and a weight. Cool thoroughly and then refrigerate, with the weight still in position, for at least 12 hours before serving. Turn out of the tin and slice before serving.

Chicken liver and brandy pâté; Sage, liver and onion

Kidney casserole

METRIC

25 g butter or margarine
1 onion, peeled and sliced
8 pig's kidneys, skinned and
  halved
4 rashers unsmoked streaky
  bacon, rinded and chopped
1 small green pepper, cored,
  seeded and sliced
100 g button mushrooms,
  cleaned
450 ml hot brown stock or
  water and ½ beef stock cube
2 × 15 ml spoons tomato
  purée
salt
freshly ground black pepper
To finish:
2 × 5 ml spoons cornflour
little water

IMPERIAL

1 oz butter or margarine
1 onion, peeled and sliced
8 pig's kidneys, skinned and
  halved
4 rashers unsmoked streaky
  bacon, rinded and chopped
1 small green pepper, cored,
  seeded and sliced
4 oz button mushrooms,
  cleaned
¾ pint hot brown stock or
  water and ½ beef stock cube
2 tablespoons tomato purée
salt
freshly ground black pepper
To finish:
2 teaspoons cornflour
little water

H Pressure – 10 minutes

METHOD

Heat the butter or margarine in the base of the cooker.
Lightly brown the onion and lift out. Brown the kidneys
and fry the bacon. Return the onion to the cooker together
with the green pepper, mushrooms, stock or water and
stock cube, tomato purée and salt and pepper. Stir well to
remove any residues from the base of the cooker. Close the
cooker, bring to H pressure and cook for 10 minutes. Reduce
the pressure quickly. Blend the cornflour with a little water.
Return the open cooker to the heat. Add the cornflour,
stirring constantly, bring to the boil and cook until thickened.
Taste and adjust the seasoning as necessary before serving.

Above, from front: Kidneys turbigo; Kidney casserole;
Right: Creamed tripe and mushrooms

Kidneys turbigo

METRIC	IMPERIAL
25 g butter or margarine	1 oz butter or margarine
225 g thin pork sausages	8 oz thin pork sausages
8 pig's kidneys	8 pig's kidneys
100 g small onions, peeled	4 oz small onions, peeled
100 g button mushrooms, cleaned	4 oz button mushrooms, cleaned
3 × 15 ml spoons tomato purée	3 tablespoons tomato purée
150 ml dry sherry	$\frac{1}{4}$ pint dry sherry
300 ml hot brown stock or water and $\frac{1}{2}$ beef stock cube	$\frac{1}{2}$ pint hot brown stock or water and $\frac{1}{2}$ beef stock cube
salt	salt
freshly ground black pepper	freshly ground black pepper
1 × 15 ml spoon cornflour	1 tablespoon cornflour
little water	little water
1 × 15 ml spoon freshly chopped parsley	1 tablespoon freshly chopped parsley

H Pressure – 6 minutes

METHOD

Heat the butter or margarine in the cooker and fry the sausages until lightly browned. Lift out, drain well and cut the sausages into bite-size pieces. Skin the kidneys, cut into half lengthways and remove the core. Brown the kidneys in the hot butter or margarine with the onions and mushrooms. Remove the cooker from the heat and stir in the tomato purée, sherry and stock or water and stock cube. Add the sausages and a little salt and pepper. Close the cooker, bring to H pressure and cook for 6 minutes. Reduce the pressure quickly. Return the open cooker to the heat, add the cornflour blended with a little cold water. Bring to the boil, stirring constantly. Taste and adjust the seasoning as necessary. Stir in the chopped parsley just before serving.

Creamed tripe and mushrooms

METRIC	IMPERIAL
500–750 g blanched tripe (prepared by the butcher)	1–1$\frac{1}{2}$ lb blanched tripe (prepared by the butcher)
cold water	cold water
1 onion, peeled and coarsely chopped	1 onion, peeled and coarsely chopped
100 g mushrooms, cleaned and sliced	4 oz mushrooms, cleaned and sliced
300 ml white stock or water and $\frac{1}{2}$ chicken stock cube	$\frac{1}{2}$ pint white stock or water and $\frac{1}{2}$ chicken stock cube
150 ml milk	$\frac{1}{4}$ pint milk
salt	salt
freshly ground black pepper	freshly ground black pepper
Sauce:	**Sauce:**
25 g butter	1 oz butter
25 g flour	1 oz flour
4 × 15 ml spoons single cream	4 tablespoons single cream
To garnish:	**To garnish:**
grilled tomato halves	grilled tomato halves

H Pressure – 15 minutes

METHOD

Cut the tripe into thin strips. Put into the cooker with sufficient cold water to cover, bring to the boil. Drain and discard the water. Add the onion, mushrooms, stock or water and stock cube and milk to the cooker with a little salt and pepper. Close the cooker, bring to H pressure and cook for 15 minutes. Reduce the pressure quickly. Strain off and reserve the cooking liquid. Transfer the tripe and vegetables to a warmed serving dish and keep hot. Rinse and dry the cooker.

Melt the butter in the cooker, add the flour and cook for a few moments. Remove from the heat and stir in the reserved cooking liquid. Return to the heat and bring to the boil, stirring constantly. Simmer for 1 minute. Remove from the heat, stir in the cream and taste and adjust the seasoning as necessary. Serve the sauce poured over the tripe and garnish with the grilled tomato halves.

Pressed ox tongue

For parties or at Christmas it is well worth cooking an ox tongue. Even if you are out at work the pressure cooker reduces the cooking time so much that it can easily be prepared in an evening.

METRIC	IMPERIAL
1 ox tongue, weighing up to 2 kg	*1 ox tongue, weighing up to 4 lb*
cold water	*cold water*
6 black peppercorns	*6 black peppercorns*
2 bay leaves	*2 bay leaves*
1 small onion, peeled and sliced	*1 small onion, peeled and sliced*
15 g powdered gelatine	*½ oz powdered gelatine*
sliced tomatoes and cucumber for garnish	*sliced tomatoes and cucumber for garnish*

H Pressure – 15 minutes per 500 g/1 lb

METHOD

Soak a salted tongue in cold water for several hours or overnight, drain and discard the water. Put the tongue into the cooker, cover with cold water, add the peppercorns, which have been crushed in a paper bag with a rolling pin, bay leaves and onion. Close the cooker, bring to H pressure and cook for the calculated time. Reduce the pressure quickly and transfer the tongue to a bowl of cold water. When cool enough to handle, peel off the skin beginning at the tip end of the tongue. Remove the bones and gristle from the root end of the tongue and trim off any loose pieces of meat. Form the tongue into a round and press into a round deep dish or cake tin. The tongue should be a tight fit as this will help in the pressing. Strain the cooking liquid and reserve 300 ml/½ pint. Dissolve the gelatine in 2 × 15 ml spoons/ 2 tablespoons of reserved cooking liquid. Bring the remaining cooking liquid to the boil, stir in the gelatine and boil for a few minutes. Pour over the tongue, cover with a piece of greaseproof paper, a plate and a heavy weight. Leave to set.

To serve: turn out and garnish with overlapping slices of tomato and cucumber.

Devilled lambs' tongues

METRIC	IMPERIAL
8 lambs' tongues	*8 lambs' tongues*
25 g lard or margarine	*1 oz lard or margarine*
1 large onion, peeled and coarsely chopped	*1 large onion, peeled and coarsely chopped*
1 large green pepper, cored, seeded and chopped	*1 large green pepper, cored, seeded and chopped*
600 ml hot brown stock or water and ½ beef stock cube	*1 pint hot brown stock or water and ½ beef stock cube*
2 × 15 ml spoons tomato purée	*2 tablespoons tomato purée*
2 × 5 ml spoons mustard powder	*2 teaspoons mustard powder*
2 × 5 ml spoons Worcestershire sauce	*2 teaspoons Worcestershire sauce*
salt	*salt*
freshly ground black pepper	*freshly ground black pepper*
1 × 5 ml spoon cornflour	*1 teaspoon cornflour*
little water	*little water*
1 × 15 ml spoon freshly chopped parsley	*1 tablespoon freshly chopped parsley*

H Pressure – 20 minutes

METHOD

Soak the tongues in cold water for several hours or overnight. Heat the lard or margarine in the cooker and lightly fry the onion and green pepper. Lift out and drain off the excess lard or margarine from the cooker. Add the stock or water and stock cube, tomato purée, mustard powder, Worcestershire sauce and a little salt and pepper to the cooker. Stir well to remove any residues from the base of the cooker. Return the vegetables and the drained tongues to the cooker. Close the cooker, bring to H pressure and cook for 20 minutes. Reduce the pressure quickly. Lift out the tongues and cool slightly before removing the skin, small bones and gristle at the root end. Blend the cornflour with a little cold water and add to the sauce. Return the open cooker to the heat and cook, stirring constantly, until boiling and thickened. Taste and adjust the seasoning as necessary. Cut the tongues into thick slices and return to the cooker to reheat. Serve sprinkled liberally with chopped parsley.

Pressed ox tongue

Oxtail ragoût

METRIC	IMPERIAL
25 g lard or margarine	1 oz lard or margarine
1 oxtail, chopped into pieces and trimmed	1 oxtail, chopped into pieces and trimmed
1 large onion, peeled and sliced	1 large onion, peeled and sliced
100 g unsmoked streaky bacon, rinded and chopped	4 oz unsmoked streaky bacon, rinded and chopped
1 garlic clove, crushed	1 garlic clove, crushed
225 g carrots, scraped and sliced	8 oz carrots, scraped and sliced
300 ml hot brown stock or water and ½ beef stock cube	½ pint hot brown stock or water and ½ beef stock cube
300 ml red wine (Burgundy-type)	½ pint red wine (Burgundy-type)
1 × 2.5 ml spoon dried marjoram	½ teaspoon dried marjoram
salt	salt
freshly ground black pepper	freshly ground black pepper
1 × 15 ml spoon flour	1 tablespoon flour
little water	little water
freshly chopped parsley	freshly chopped parsley

From front: Devilled lambs' tongues; Oxtail ragoût

H Pressure – 40 minutes

METHOD

Heat the lard or margarine in the cooker, add the oxtail and sauté until well browned all over. Lift out and drain well. Fry the onion, bacon, garlic and carrots, for 2 to 3 minutes. Lift out and drain off the excess lard or margarine from the cooker. Away from the heat, add the stock or water and stock cube and wine to the cooker and stir well to remove any residues from the base of the cooker. Return the oxtail and vegetable mixture to the cooker together with the marjoram and salt and pepper. Close the cooker, bring to H pressure and cook for 40 minutes. Reduce the pressure quickly. Lift out the oxtail to a warmed dish and keep hot.

Return the open cooker to the heat and stir in the flour blended with a little cold water. Stir constantly until the sauce boils and thickens. Taste and adjust the seasoning as necessary before pouring over the oxtail. Garnish liberally with freshly chopped parsley.

One-pot Meals

The object of this section is to show the variety of dishes that can be planned and cooked in the one-pot way – either cooking everything at one time or adding vegetables or other accompaniments part-way through the cooking.

The recipes in this section do not try to cook a main course and dessert together – although it can be done. But for family-sized meals there is probably not going to be room in your pressure cooker anyway!

However, because cooking times are so short, there is no reason why, with a little forward planning, the dessert should not be cooked first or, alternatively, be left to cook while you are eating the main course.

If you are adding vegetables during the cooking, and intend to serve them separately, it is advisable to line the trivet or separator with a piece of greaseproof paper. This will prevent the vegetables from becoming stained with the gravy or sauce from the meat. Add 1 minute to the cooking time you are allowing for the vegetables if you have a solid separator, or if you use aluminium foil instead as neither of these permit the steam to penetrate so quickly and readily. Apart from the obvious fuel savings, this method of planning and cooking your meals reduces washing-up to a minimum.

Pot roast of brisket

Served with boiled potatoes and green beans.

METRIC
1 kg piece of rolled brisket
25 g flour
salt
freshly ground black pepper
50 g lard or margarine
1 large onion, peeled and
  sliced
2 large carrots, scraped and
  sliced
600 ml hot brown stock or
  water and ½ beef stock cube
2 × 15 ml spoons tomato
  purée
bouquet garni
500 g potatoes, peeled and
  quartered if large
500 g packet frozen green
  beans or fresh beans

IMPERIAL
2 lb piece of rolled brisket
1 oz flour
salt
freshly ground black pepper
2 oz lard or margarine
1 large onion, peeled and
  sliced
2 large carrots, scraped and
  sliced
1 pint hot brown stock or
  water and ½ beef stock cube
2 tablespoons tomato purée
bouquet garni
1 lb potatoes, peeled and
  quartered if large
1 lb packet frozen green
  beans or fresh beans

Pot roast of brisket ; Beef risotto

H Pressure – 40 minutes

METHOD
Coat the meat in the flour seasoned with salt and pepper. Heat the lard or margarine in the cooker and brown the meat on all sides. Add the onion and carrots and fry lightly. Lift out the meat and vegetables and drain the excess lard or margarine from the cooker. Add the stock or water and stock cube, tomato purée and bouquet garni to the cooker. Stir well to remove any residues from the base of the cooker. Put the trivet into the cooker, stand the joint on the trivet and surround the joint with the vegetables. Close the cooker, bring to H pressure and cook for 35 minutes. Reduce the pressure quickly. Move the meat over to one side of the cooker and add the lightly salted potatoes. If liked wrap the potatoes in a piece of greaseproof paper if you do not want them to absorb any sauce. Bring the liquid back to the boil and add a separator containing the lightly salted beans. Close the cooker, bring to H pressure and cook for a further 5 minutes. Reduce the pressure quickly.

Lift out the beans and potatoes and keep hot. Lift out the meat, remove the string, slice and keep hot. Remove the trivet and bouquet garni from the cooker. Mash the onion and carrots into the sauce and serve over the sliced meat with the potatoes and beans. Hand any extra sauce separately.

Beef risotto

METRIC	IMPERIAL
25 g butter or margarine	1 oz butter or margarine
1 small onion, peeled and coarsely chopped	1 small onion, peeled and coarsely chopped
1 small green pepper, cored, seeded and coarsely chopped	1 small green pepper, cored, seeded and coarsely chopped
350 g minced beef	12 oz minced beef
100 g mushrooms, washed and coarsely chopped	4 oz mushrooms, washed and coarsely chopped
225 g long-grain rice	8 oz long-grain rice
600 ml brown stock or water and ½ beef stock cube	1 pint brown stock or water and ½ beef stock cube
1 × 5 ml spoon Worcestershire sauce	1 teaspoon Worcestershire sauce
salt	salt
freshly ground black pepper	freshly ground black pepper
2 × 15 ml spoons chopped parsley	2 tablespoons chopped parsley
25 g Parmesan cheese	1 oz Parmesan cheese

H Pressure – 6 minutes

METHOD

Heat the butter or margarine in the cooker and fry the onion and green pepper until both are beginning to soften. Add the beef and fry until lightly browned. Carefully drain off any excess butter or margarine from the cooker. Return the cooker to the heat and add the mushrooms, rice, stock or water and stock cube, Worcestershire sauce and salt and pepper. Stir well to remove any residues from the base of the cooker. Close the cooker, bring to H pressure and cook for 6 minutes. Reduce the pressure quickly. Return the open cooker to a low heat and stir with a fork to separate the rice grains. Stir in the parsley and taste and adjust the seasoning as necessary. Serve sprinkled with finely grated Parmesan cheese.

Beef stew with parsley dumplings

METRIC	IMPERIAL
50 g lard or margarine	2 oz lard or margarine
750 g stewing beef, trimmed and cut into 2.5 cm chunks	1½ lb stewing beef, trimmed and cut into 1 inch chunks
1 large onion, peeled and sliced	1 large onion, peeled and sliced
4 celery stalks, scrubbed and roughly chopped	4 celery stalks, scrubbed and roughly chopped
4 carrots, peeled and sliced	4 carrots, peeled and sliced
600 ml hot brown stock or water and ½ beef stock cube	1 pint hot brown stock or water and ½ beef stock cube
salt	salt
freshly ground black pepper	freshly ground black pepper
1 bouquet garni	1 bouquet garni

For dumplings:	For dumplings:
175 g self-raising flour	6 oz self-raising flour
1 × 2.5 ml spoon salt	½ teaspoon salt
75 g shredded beef suet	3 oz shredded beef suet
1 × 15 ml spoon freshly chopped parsley	1 tablespoon freshly chopped parsley
6 × 15 ml spoons cold water	6 tablespoons cold water

H Pressure – 20 minutes

METHOD

Heat the lard or margarine in the cooker and sauté the beef until evenly browned. Remove the meat from the cooker and drain well. Fry the vegetables until they are beginning to colour. Remove the cooker from the heat, stir in the hot stock or water and stock cube to remove any residues from the base of the cooker. Return the meat to the cooker with salt, pepper and bouquet garni. Close the cooker, bring to H pressure and cook for 20 minutes. Reduce the pressure quickly and remove the bouquet garni.

While the meat is cooking, prepare the dumplings. Sift the flour and salt into a mixing bowl, stir in the shredded suet and parsley. Mix with the water until a smooth elastic dough is formed that leaves the sides of the bowl cleanly. Turn on to a floured board, knead lightly and divide into 8 pieces. Shape into balls. When the stew is cooked, return the open cooker to the heat and drop the dumplings into the boiling gravy. Place the cover over the cooker to form a lid, but do not close or add weight. Simmer gently for 10 minutes.

Beef stew with parsley dumplings

Beef curry with saffron rice

METRIC	IMPERIAL
3 × 15 ml spoons vegetable oil	3 tablespoons vegetable oil
1 large onion, peeled and coarsely chopped	1 large onion, peeled and coarsely chopped
750 g stewing beef, trimmed and cut into 2.5 cm cubes	1½ lb stewing beef, trimmed and cut into 1 inch cubes
Curry spices:	**Curry spices:**
2 × 15 ml spoons ground cumin	2 tablespoons ground cumin
1 × 15 ml spoon ground coriander	1 tablespoon ground coriander
1 × 5 ml spoon ground turmeric	1 teaspoon ground turmeric
2 × 5 ml spoons chilli powder	2 teaspoons chilli powder
1 × 2.5 ml spoon ground ginger	½ teaspoon ground ginger
1 × 2.5 ml spoon ground fenugreek	½ teaspoon ground fenugreek

Minced beef and pasta casserole

METRIC	IMPERIAL
25 g lard or margarine	1 oz lard or margarine
1 onion, peeled and chopped	1 onion, peeled and chopped
1 garlic clove, crushed	1 garlic clove, crushed
500 g minced beef	1 lb minced beef
300 ml hot brown stock or water and ½ beef stock cube	½ pint hot brown stock or water and ½ beef stock cube
1 × 225 g can tomatoes	1 × 8 oz can tomatoes
1 × 219 g can baked beans	1 × 7¾ oz can baked beans
1 × 2.5 ml spoon dried mixed herbs	½ teaspoon dried mixed herbs
2 × 5 ml spoons paprika pepper	2 teaspoons paprika pepper
2 × 5 ml spoons Worcestershire sauce	2 teaspoons Worcestershire sauce
75 g pasta whirls or shells	3 oz pasta whirls or shells
salt	salt
freshly ground black pepper	freshly ground black pepper
freshly chopped parsley	freshly chopped parsley

H Pressure – 7 minutes

METHOD

Heat the lard or margarine in the cooker, add the onion and garlic and fry until the onion is beginning to soften. Add the minced beef and brown quickly. Carefully drain off any excess lard or margarine from the cooker. Stir in the remaining ingredients except the salt, pepper and parsley. Season with a little salt and pepper. Close the cooker, bring to H pressure and cook for 7 minutes. Reduce the pressure quickly. Taste and adjust the seasoning as necessary. Serve garnished with a little chopped parsley.

750 ml hot brown stock or water and ½ beef stock cube	1¼ pints hot brown stock or water and ½ beef stock cube
1 × 15 ml spoon tomato purée	1 tablespoon tomato purée
50 g sultanas (optional)	2 oz sultanas (optional)
a little salt	a little salt
225 g long-grain patna rice	8 oz long-grain patna rice
450 ml water	¾ pint water
good pinch powdered saffron	good pinch powdered saffron
salt	salt
1 × 15 ml spoon cornflour	1 tablespoon cornflour
little water	little water

H Pressure – 20 minutes

METHOD

Heat the oil in the cooker. Fry the onion and beef until lightly browned. Mix together all the curry spices and stir into the meat and onion. Cook gently for 2 to 3 minutes. Away from the heat add the stock or water and stock cube, tomato purée and sultanas if used. Stir well to remove any residues from the base of the cooker. Return to the heat, bring to the boil and add a little salt. Close the cooker, bring to H pressure and cook for 15 minutes. Reduce the pressure quickly. Stir the curry mixture. Add the trivet and an oven-proof dish containing the rice, water, saffron and salt, cover the dish with a piece of greaseproof paper. Close the cooker, bring to H pressure and cook for a further 5 minutes. Reduce the pressure slowly. Lift out the dish of rice, transfer to a strainer and rinse with boiling water. Keep hot.

Return the open cooker to the heat. Stir in the cornflour blended with a little cold water and cook, stirring constantly, until thickened. Taste and adjust the seasoning as necessary. Serve the curry on a bed of the rice with a selection of accompaniments.

Suggested accompaniments:

Mango chutney.

Thinly sliced green peppers and sliced raw mushrooms.

Bananas, peeled and sliced and topped with a little lemon juice.

Peeled and diced cucumber mixed with natural yoghurt.

This recipe can also be used for cubed lamb or pork – allow 15 minutes cooking time, or chicken pieces – allow 6 minutes cooking time.

Left: Minced beef and pasta casserole; Below: Beef curry with saffron rice

Barbecued pork chops with orange rice

METRIC	IMPERIAL
25 g lard or margarine	1 oz lard or margarine
4 pork chops	4 pork chops
1 small onion, peeled and chopped	1 small onion, peeled and chopped
450 ml hot brown stock or water and ½ beef stock cube	¾ pint hot brown stock or water and ½ beef stock cube
1 × 15 ml spoon tomato purée	1 tablespoon tomato purée
3 × 15 ml spoons vinegar	3 tablespoons vinegar
2 × 15 ml spoons demerara sugar	2 tablespoons demerara sugar
1 × 5 ml spoon mustard powder	1 teaspoon mustard powder
1 × 5 ml spoon Worcestershire sauce	1 teaspoon Worcestershire sauce
salt	salt
freshly ground black pepper	freshly ground black pepper
225 g easy-cook, long-grain rice	8 oz easy-cook, long-grain rice
300 ml canned unsweetened orange juice	½ pint canned unsweetened orange juice
150 ml water	¼ pint water
1 × 15 ml spoon cornflour	1 tablespoon cornflour
little water	little water
1 fresh orange for garnish	1 fresh orange for garnish

H Pressure – 10 minutes

METHOD

Heat the lard or margarine in the cooker, brown the chops on both sides, remove from the cooker and fry the onion lightly. Lift out and drain the excess lard or margarine from the cooker. Put the onion back into the cooker with the stock or water and stock cube, tomato purée, vinegar, sugar, mustard powder and Worcestershire sauce. Stir well to remove any residues from the base of the cooker. Put the trivet into the cooker, place the chops on top and season lightly with salt and pepper. Close the cooker, bring to H pressure and cook for 4 minutes. Reduce the pressure quickly. Stand an ovenproof dish or solid separator containing the rice, orange juice, water and a little salt on top of the chops. Cover with a piece of greaseproof paper. Close the cooker, bring to H pressure and cook for 6 minutes. Reduce the pressure slowly. Lift out the rice, stir with a fork to separate the grains and transfer to a warmed serving dish. Keep hot. Place the chops on the rice. Remove the trivet, return the open cooker to the heat and add the cornflour blended with a little water. Bring to the boil and stir continuously until thickened. Taste and adjust the seasoning as necessary. Pour the sauce over the chops and garnish with slices of orange.

Liver and bacon

Served with creamed potatoes and mixed vegetables.

METRIC	IMPERIAL
500–750 g lamb's or pig's liver, cut into 1 cm slices	1–1½ lb lamb's or pig's liver, cut into ½ inch slices
25 g flour	1 oz flour
salt	salt
freshly ground black pepper	freshly ground black pepper
50 g lard or margarine	2 oz lard or margarine
1 small onion, peeled and chopped	1 small onion, peeled and chopped
450 ml hot brown stock or water and ½ beef stock cube	¾ pint hot brown stock or water and ½ beef stock cube
8 rashers unsmoked back bacon, rinded	8 rashers unsmoked back bacon, rinded
500 g potatoes, peeled and quartered if large	1 lb potatoes, peeled and quartered if large
1 × 500 g packet frozen mixed vegetables	1 × 1 lb packet frozen mixed vegetables
little butter and milk	little butter and milk

H Pressure – 5 minutes

METHOD

Coat the liver in the flour seasoned with a little salt and pepper and shake well to remove any excess. Heat the lard or margarine in the cooker and fry the liver lightly on both sides with the onion. Lift out and drain the excess lard or margarine from the cooker. Add the stock or water and stock cube to the cooker and stir well to remove any residues from the base of the cooker. Replace the liver and onion and lay the bacon rashers over the top. Cover with the trivet and a piece of greaseproof paper and add the potatoes sprinkled with a little salt. Bring the liquid in the cooker to the boil and add a separator containing the lightly salted frozen mixed vegetables. Close the cooker, bring to H pressure and cook for 5 minutes. Reduce the pressure quickly. Lift out the mixed vegetables and keep hot. Transfer the potatoes to a bowl and mash with a little butter, salt and pepper and milk. Lift out the liver and bacon and thicken the gravy if necessary with a little blended flour.

Barbecued pork chops with orange rice

West country collar

Cider gives a delicious flavour to this bacon collar joint and is served with a selection of root vegetables and buttered cabbage.

METRIC	IMPERIAL
1 kg collar joint of bacon	*2 lb collar joint of bacon*
cold water	*cold water*
600 ml dry cider	*1 pint dry cider*
2 large leeks, washed and cut into large pieces	*2 large leeks, washed and cut into large pieces*
2 large carrots, scraped and quartered	*2 large carrots, scraped and quartered*
2 parsnips, peeled and quartered	*2 parsnips, peeled and quartered*
salt	*salt*
freshly ground black pepper	*freshly ground black pepper*
1 medium cabbage, washed and shredded	*1 medium cabbage, washed and shredded*
little butter	*little butter*
1 × 15 ml spoon flour	*1 tablespoon flour*
little water	*little water*

Liver and bacon ; West country collar

H Pressure – 24 minutes

METHOD

Put the bacon into the cooker, cover with cold water and bring to the boil in the open cooker. Lift out the bacon and discard the water. Put the trivet into the cooker, stand the bacon on the trivet and pour the cider over. Put the leeks, carrots and parsnips around the bacon and season lightly with salt and pepper. Close the cooker, bring to H pressure and cook for 20 minutes. Reduce the pressure quickly. Stand a separator, containing the lightly salted cabbage on top of the joint. Close the cooker, bring to H pressure and cook for 4 minutes. Reduce the pressure quickly. Lift out the cabbage, transfer to a warmed serving dish and toss with a little pepper and butter. Keep hot. Lift out the vegetables and bacon. Remove the string and rind and slice the bacon thickly. Lift the trivet out and return the open cooker to the heat. Add the flour blended with a little water and stir constantly until the sauce is boiling and thickened. Taste and adjust the seasoning as necessary and pour the sauce over the sliced bacon. Garnish with the cooked root vegetables and serve with the cabbage. Hand any extra sauce separately.

Hasty chicken

A can of cook-in-wine sauce provides the basis for this tasty dish. The accompanying vegetables are steamed potatoes and buttered courgettes.

METRIC	IMPERIAL
4 × 15 ml spoons oil	4 tablespoons oil
1 onion, peeled and chopped	1 onion, peeled and chopped
100 g button mushrooms, cleaned	4 oz button mushrooms, cleaned
4 chicken portions, skinned	4 chicken portions, skinned
1 × 376 g can red wine sauce	1 × 13¼ oz can red wine sauce
150 ml water	¼ pint water
salt	salt
500 g potatoes, peeled and quartered if large	1 lb potatoes, peeled and quartered if large
500 g courgettes, washed and thickly sliced	1 lb courgettes, washed and thickly sliced
a little butter	a little butter
freshly chopped parsley	freshly chopped parsley
freshly ground black pepper	freshly ground black pepper

H Pressure – 5 minutes

METHOD

Heat the oil in the cooker, add the onion and mushrooms and sauté for a few moments without colouring. Lift out. Add the chicken to the hot oil and brown evenly on both sides. Lift out and drain well. Drain the excess oil from the cooker. Away from the heat add the can of sauce and water. Stir well to remove any residues from the base of the cooker. Return the chicken and vegetables to the cooker. Cover the chicken with the trivet and a piece of greaseproof paper and add the lightly salted potatoes. Return the cooker to the heat and bring the sauce to the boil, so that the cooker is filled with steam. Stand a separator, containing the lightly salted courgettes on top of the potatoes. Close the cooker, bring to H pressure and cook for 5 minutes. Reduce the pressure quickly. Lift out the courgettes and transfer to a warmed serving dish with a little butter. Serve the potatoes with a little butter and chopped parsley. Lift out the chicken, taste and adjust the seasoning of the sauce before serving.

Hasty chicken; Sweet and sour chicken with noodles

Fish pie

Sweet and sour chicken with noodles

METRIC	IMPERIAL
2 × 15 ml spoons cooking oil	2 tablespoons cooking oil
4 breasts of chicken, skinned	4 breasts of chicken, skinned
1 small onion, peeled and chopped	1 small onion, peeled and chopped
1 small green pepper, cored, seeded and sliced	1 small green pepper, cored, seeded and sliced
1 × 280 g can pineapple cubes	1 × 10 oz can pineapple cubes
2 × 15 ml spoons pineapple juice	2 tablespoons pineapple juice
2 × 15 ml spoons tomato purée	2 tablespoons tomato purée
1 × 15 ml spoon demerara sugar	1 tablespoon demerara sugar
1 × 5 ml spoon ground ginger	1 teaspoon ground ginger
2 × 15 ml spoons vinegar	2 tablespoons vinegar
300 ml hot brown stock or water and ½ beef stock cube	½ pint hot brown stock or water and ½ beef stock cube
1 × 5 ml spoon soy sauce	1 teaspoon soy sauce
350 g noodles	12 oz noodles
300 ml cold water	½ pint cold water
little butter	little butter
2 × 5 ml spoons cornflour	2 teaspoons cornflour
little water	little water

H Pressure – 5 minutes

METHOD

Heat the oil in the cooker and brown the chicken on both sides. Lift the chicken out and drain the excess oil from the cooker. Put all the other ingredients except the noodles, water, butter, cornflour and little water into the cooker. Add the trivet and lay the chicken pieces on top. Stand an oven-proof dish or solid separator containing the noodles and lightly salted water on top of the chicken. Cover with a piece of greaseproof paper. Close the cooker, bring to H pressure and cook for 5 minutes. Reduce the pressure quickly. Lift out the noodles, drain, add a little butter and toss lightly. Transfer to a warmed serving dish and keep hot. Lift out the chicken and place on top of the noodles. Remove the trivet, return open cooker to the heat and add the corn-flour blended with a little water. Bring to the boil stirring constantly. Taste and adjust the seasoning as necessary. Serve the sauce over the chicken and hand any extra separately.

Fish pie

METRIC	IMPERIAL
1 small onion, peeled and chopped	1 small onion, peeled and chopped
1 bay leaf	1 bay leaf
300 ml water	½ pint water
little butter or margarine for greasing	little butter or margarine for greasing
750 g haddock fillets	1½ lb haddock fillets
100 g button mushrooms, cleaned	4 oz button mushrooms, cleaned
750 g potatoes, peeled and thickly sliced	1½ lb potatoes, peeled and thickly sliced
a little salt	a little salt
15 g butter	½ oz butter
a little milk	a little milk
2 eggs, hard-boiled	2 eggs, hard-boiled
Sauce:	**Sauce:**
25 g butter or margarine	1 oz butter or margarine
25 g flour	1 oz flour
300 ml milk	½ pint milk
salt	salt
freshly ground black pepper	freshly ground black pepper
a little freshly chopped parsley (optional)	a little freshly chopped parsley (optional)

H Pressure – 5 minutes

METHOD

Put the onion, bay leaf and water into the cooker. Grease the trivet with a little butter or margarine and place in the cooker. Put the fish on the trivet. Place the button mushrooms to one side of the fish. Put the potatoes into a separator, sprinkle with a little salt and stand on top of the fish. Close the cooker, bring to H pressure and cook for 5 minutes. Reduce the pressure quickly. Lift out the potatoes, transfer to a bowl and mash with the butter and milk. Remove the fish and cut into thick strips. Lift out the mushrooms and combine with the fish. Strain off the cooking liquid, reserving 150 ml/¼ pint for the sauce. Mix the onion with the fish and discard the bay leaf. Rinse and dry the cooker.

Melt the butter or margarine in the open cooker. Stir in the flour and cook for a few moments. Remove from the heat and add the milk and reserved cooking liquid. Return to the heat and bring to the boil, stirring constantly. Cook for 1 minute and taste and adjust the seasoning as necessary. Put the fish mixture into a 1.2 litre/2 pint pie dish. Shell and quarter the eggs and layer over the fish. Pour over the sauce and finally cover with the mashed potato. Place under a hot grill to brown and crisp the potato. Sprinkle with a little chopped parsley before serving, if liked.

Desserts

I have heard it said that one of the best reasons for using a pressure cooker is for the delicious steamed puddings it cooks – the variety we used to enjoy a few years ago, but which, with the faster pace of life, have often been pushed aside for the quicker convenience instant desserts.

Favourites such as treacle pudding, spotted dog and jam roly poly are almost as much a part of our cookery heritage as roast beef, but without several hours of cooking and the accompanying steam, how do you cook them? Very simply and quickly when you use a pressure cooker.

In the same way, but at the other end of the scale, light egg custards and delicious crème caramels can be cooked in just a few minutes. Like many desserts, custards can be flavoured to suit your particular taste. Custards and crème desserts are probably more popular in the spring and summer months and are delicious with fresh fruit. In this way your pressure cooker can be of service all year round.

When the appearance of cooked fruit is important, such as for flans or tarts, there are few better or quicker way of cooking the fruit than in a pressure cooker. Generally it is best to cook such fruits, for example apricots, plums and rhubarb, with a very little water in an ovenproof container in the pressure cooker. The resulting liquid will be almost pure fruit juice and can be made into a sauce or glaze.

General instructions for steamed puddings

1. Use L (5 lb or 7½ lb) pressure for all puddings, as this will give a lighter more open-textured result. For L (7½ lb) pressure cookers use the same cooking times given for L (5 lb) pressure. H (15 lb) pressure can be used for suet puddings, but if you only have a fixed weight on your cooker, steamed sponge puddings will give better results if made into individual puddings. Alternatively, if you have a fixed weight cooker and intend to cook a lot of puddings, one manufacturer offers a replacement set of weights, converting a fixed weight to a set of three.

2. The trivet is always used in the base of the cooker. If you are cooking two puddings (one on top of the other) in a larger cooker, then the trivet will be used as a shelf between the basins.

3. There must always be at least 900 ml/1½ pints boiling water in the cooker before cooking commences. This volume is required to cover the small loss of liquid during the steaming period prior to pressure cooking and ensures that there will be sufficient liquid left for the pressure cooking. To ensure that none of the water is evaporated before cooking commences, add boiling water from a kettle just as the pudding is ready to be cooked – do not leave the open cooker bubbling away while you make the pudding. To prevent discoloration of aluminium cookers in hard water areas, add one tablespoon of vinegar or lemon juice to the liquid.

4. The cooking container or basin *must* be heatproof. In the case of plastic or polythene basins do ensure that these are guaranteed to be of a boilable material. The majority of basins on the market are

ovenproof glass or china and this type have been used for testing the recipes in this section. Enamel, metal or aluminium foil basins make for slightly quicker cooking. Therefore, if you use one of these materials, reduce the pressure cooking time by 3 minutes for individual puddings and 5 minutes for a larger pudding. The basin should always be greased and no more than two-thirds full with the uncooked mixture.

5. All puddings must be covered, either by a double thickness of greased greaseproof paper or a single piece of greased aluminium foil. Make a pleat across the centre to allow space for the pudding to rise. Tie down with string, but leave a sufficiently long piece of string to secure across the top of the pudding to form a lifting handle. When using foil, fold two long strips several times and place these under the pudding, using the ends for lifting.

6. Steamed puddings are cooked and timed in two stages:
   a) Steaming. This is done over a low heat with the cover in position but *not* the weights. (In the case of the fixed lever style weight it is left in the upright position.) During steaming there should only be a slight escape of steam through the centre vent.
   b) At the completion of the steaming period the weight is added and the heat increased so that the cooker is brought quickly to pressure. The heat is then lowered again and the pudding cooked for the appropriate time.

7. After cooking allow the pressure to reduce *slowly* – this will usually take 10 to 15 minutes.

8. Your own favourite recipes can be adapted for pressure cooking and the times required will be considerably shorter. As a guide:

NORMAL COOKING TIME	IN THE PRESSURE COOKER	
	STEAMING	L (5 lb) PRESSURE
Sponge puddings		
30 minutes	**5 minutes**	10 minutes
1 to 1½ hours	**15 minutes**	25 to 30 minutes
Suet puddings in a basin		
1½ to 2 hours	**15 minutes**	40 minutes
Suet puddings in a roll		
1½ to 2 hours	**10 minutes**	25 to 30 minutes

Christmas pudding – see recipe, page 131.
This guideline is given for puddings using a 900 m/1½ pint pudding basin. Larger quantities will require longer cooking times. Allow approximately 10 minutes longer pressure cooking for each additional 50 g/2 oz flour. (The other ingredients will generally be increased proportionally.) Remember to add more liquid for longer cooking times – a further 150 ml/¼ pint is required for each additional 15 minutes of cooking.

Steamed puddings for the home freezer
Suet puddings
These are better if frozen in the uncooked state and then thawed before cooking in the usual way. This also applies to savoury suet puddings.

Sponge puddings
These can either be cooked and then frozen, or frozen in an uncooked state.
Cooked sponge puddings – To reheat from frozen cover the pudding with greaseproof paper or foil. Put 600 ml/1 pint water into the cooker, with a little lemon juice or vinegar. Stand the pudding on the trivet and bring to H pressure. Allow 20 minutes for individual puddings and 25 to 30 minutes for larger puddings. Reduce pressure quickly.
Uncooked sponge puddings – Cover the frozen pudding with greaseproof paper or foil. Put 1.2 litres/2 pints boiling water into the cooker, with a little lemon juice or vinegar. Stand the pudding on the trivet and steam for 15 minutes longer than recommended for the recipe, pressure cook for the same time given in the recipe. Reduce pressure slowly.

General instructions for fresh fruits

1. Place the trivet in the cooker with 300 ml/½ pint water and a little lemon juice or vinegar.

2. Put the fruit into a heatproof container. For soft fruits such as apples, blackberries, gooseberries and rhubarb, layer the fruit with sugar to taste and add 1 × 15 ml spoon/1 tablespoon water. For stone fruits such as apricots, greengages and plums, layer the fruit with sugar to taste and add 2 × 15 ml spoons/2 tablespoons water. Cover the container with greaseproof paper or foil.
3. Stand the container on the trivet and bring to H pressure. Cook for the recommended time. See chart below.
4. Reduce pressure quickly.

Stewing fruit for pies and purees

When stewing fruit for pies or purées, as it is not important to retain the shape of the fruit, it may be cooked directly in the base of the cooker with a minimum of 300 ml/$\frac{1}{2}$ pint water or sugar syrup. For the sugar syrup dissolve 100 g/4 oz sugar in 300 ml/$\frac{1}{2}$ pint water, boil for 1 minute and use as liked.

The pressure cooker must be no more than half full when all the fruit and liquid have been added. If you are going to use the fruit as a purée, reduce the cooking times given in the chart by 1 minute and allow the pressure to reduce slowly. If you wish the fruit to be a little firmer, cook for the recommended time then reduce pressure quickly. When the fruit is cooked, use as desired.

Fresh fruit cooking times

All times given below are for fruits cooked in a heatproof container, unless otherwise specified.

FRUIT	PREPARA-TION	H (15 lb) PRESSURE	L (7$\frac{1}{2}$ lb) PRESSURE
Apples	Peel and core Quarter Sliced thickly	6 minutes 4 minutes	10 minutes 7 minutes
Apricots	Halve and stone Leave whole Prick each apricot with a fork	3 minutes 5 minutes	5 minutes 8 minutes
Blackberries	Whole	3 minutes	5 minutes
Blackcurrants	Whole	3 minutes	5 minutes
Cherries	Whole	3 minutes	5 minutes
Damsons	Halve and stone Leave whole Prick each damson with a fork	3 minutes 5 minutes	5 minutes 8 minutes
Gooseberries	Whole	4 minutes	6 minutes
Greengages	Halve and stone Leave whole Prick each greengage with a fork	3 minutes 5 minutes	5 minutes 8 minutes

FRUIT	PREPARA-TION	H (15 lb) PRESSURE	L (7$\frac{1}{2}$ lb) PRESSURE
Peaches	Plunge into boiling water for 1 minute Cool and remove skins Halve and stone Slice	4 minutes 3 minutes	6 minutes 5 minutes
Pears Dessert pears Stewing pears	Peel, halve and core Halve Cook directly in base of cooker with sugar syrup Cooking time depends on hardness	5 minutes 6–8 minutes	8 minutes 9–12 minutes
Plums	Halve and stone Leave whole Prick each plum with a fork	3 minutes 5 minutes	5 minutes 8 minutes
Rhubarb	Cut into 2.5 cm/1 inch lengths	5 minutes	7 minutes

General instructions for dried fruits

1. All dried fruits must be soaked before pressure cooking. Place the fruit in a basin and add boiling water, allowing 600 ml/1 pint for each 500 g/1 lb of fruit. Leave to soak for a minimum of 10 minutes.
2. Transfer the fruit and soaking liquid to the cooker, without the trivet and add a little sugar or honey to sweeten. Do not have the cooker more than half full.
3. Bring to H pressure and cook for the recommended time then reduce the pressure *slowly*.

Dried fruit cooking times

FRUIT	H (15 lb) PRESSURE	L (7$\frac{1}{2}$ lb) PRESSURE
Apple rings	5 minutes	7$\frac{1}{2}$ minutes
Apricots	5 minutes	7$\frac{1}{2}$ minutes
Figs	10 minutes	15 minutes
Mixed fruit	10 minutes	15 minutes
Peaches	5 minutes	7$\frac{1}{2}$ minutes
Pears	10 minutes	15 minutes
Prunes	10 minutes	15 minutes

For extra flavour add one or two cloves to apples; a piece of lemon or orange peel to apricots, peaches, figs or pears; or substitute one or two tablespoons water with fresh orange or lemon juice for any of the fruits.

Lemon sponge puddings

METRIC	IMPERIAL
little butter or margarine for greasing	little butter or margarine for greasing
4 heaped 5 ml spoons lemon curd	4 heaped teaspoons lemon curd
100 g butter or margarine	4 oz butter or margarine
100 g caster sugar	4 oz caster sugar
finely grated rind of 1 lemon	finely grated rind of 1 lemon
2 eggs, beaten	2 eggs, beaten
100 g self-raising flour, sifted	4 oz self-raising flour, sifted
2 × 15 ml spoons lemon juice	2 tablespoons lemon juice
900 ml boiling water	1½ pints boiling water
little lemon juice	little lemon juice
Sauce:	**Sauce:**
6 × 15 ml spoons lemon curd	6 tablespoons lemon curd
2 × 15 ml spoons lemon juice	2 tablespoons lemon juice

Steaming – 5 minutes
L Pressure – 10 minutes OR
H Pressure – 7 minutes

METHOD

Grease four large teacups with a little butter or margarine. Place 1 heaped 5 ml spoon/1 heaped teaspoon of lemon curd into each teacup. Cream the butter or margarine, sugar and lemon rind together until light and fluffy. Beat in the eggs, a little at a time. Fold in the flour and finally the lemon juice. Divide the mixture between the cups, cover each with a double thickness of greased greaseproof paper or a piece of greased aluminium foil and tie down. Have the water and lemon juice boiling in the cooker and add the trivet, rim side down. Stand the puddings on the trivet, close the cooker and steam for 5 minutes. Bring to L or H pressure and cook for 10 or 7 minutes accordingly, then reduce the pressure slowly. While the pressure is reducing make the sauce. Heat the lemon curd and lemon juice gently and pour over the turned out puddings.

Cherry and almond pudding

METRIC	IMPERIAL
little butter or margarine for greasing	little butter or margarine for greasing
2 × 15 ml spoons brown sugar	2 tablespoons brown sugar
50 g butter	2 oz butter
1 × 425 g can red cherries, drained and pitted	1 × 15 oz can red cherries, drained and pitted
100 g butter or margarine	4 oz butter or margarine
100 g caster sugar	4 oz caster sugar
2 eggs, beaten	2 eggs, beaten
75 g self-raising flour, sifted	3 oz self-raising flour, sifted
25 g ground almonds	1 oz ground almonds
1 × 5 ml spoon almond essence	1 teaspoon almond essence
900 ml boiling water	1½ pints boiling water
little lemon juice	little lemon juice

Steaming – 15 minutes
L Pressure – 25 minutes

METHOD

Grease a 1.2 litre/2 pint soufflé dish or similar straight-sided ovenproof dish that will fit easily into your cooker with a little butter or margarine. Put the brown sugar and butter into a saucepan and melt over a low heat, pour into the soufflé dish. Top with a layer of the cherries.

Cream the butter or margarine and sugar until light and fluffy. Beat in the eggs, a little at a time. Fold in the flour and ground almonds and finally the almond essence. Spread the mixture over the cherries and smooth the top. Cover with a double layer of greased greaseproof paper or a piece of greased aluminium foil and tie down. Have the water and lemon juice boiling in the cooker and add the trivet, rim side down. Stand the pudding on the trivet. Close the cooker and steam, without the weights, for 15 minutes. Raise the heat and bring to L pressure. Cook for 25 minutes. Reduce the pressure slowly. Lift out the pudding and turn out on to a serving dish. Serve with whipped double cream.

Steaming – 15 minutes
L Pressure – 30 minutes

METHOD

Cream the butter or margarine and sugar until light and fluffy. Beat in the eggs, a little at a time. Fold in the flour. Carefully fold in the chopped ginger. Lightly grease a 900 ml/1½ pint pudding basin with a little butter or margarine and put in half the golden syrup. Spread the mixture over the golden syrup and smooth the top. Cover with a double layer of greased greaseproof paper or a piece of greased aluminium foil and tie down. Have the water and lemon juice boiling in the cooker and add the trivet, rim side down. Stand the pudding on the trivet, close the cooker and steam, without weights, for 15 minutes. Raise the heat, bring to L pressure and cook for 30 minutes. Reduce the pressure slowly. Turn out of the basin. Serve the pudding with the remaining golden syrup poured over and whipped double cream or ice cream.

Golden ginger pudding

METRIC	IMPERIAL
100 g butter or margarine	*4 oz butter or margarine*
100 g caster sugar	*4 oz caster sugar*
2 large eggs, beaten	*2 large eggs, beaten*
175 g self-raising flour, sifted	*6 oz self-raising flour, sifted*
25 g stem ginger, finely chopped	*1 oz stem ginger, finely chopped*
little butter or margarine for greasing	*little butter or margarine for greasing*
4 × 15 ml spoons golden syrup	*4 tablespoons golden syrup*
900 ml boiling water	*1½ pints boiling water*
little lemon juice	*little lemon juice*

Right: Golden ginger pudding; Above: Cherry and almond pudding; Lemon sponge puddings

Apple and honey pudding

METRIC	IMPERIAL
225 g self-raising flour	8 oz self-raising flour
pinch of salt	pinch of salt
100 g shredded beef suet	4 oz shredded beef suet
.. × 5 ml spoons caster sugar	2 teaspoons caster sugar
approx. 150 ml water	approx. ¼ pint water
little butter or margarine for greasing	little butter or margarine for greasing
750 g cooking apples, peeled and thinly sliced	1½ lb cooking apples, peeled and thinly sliced
4 × 15 ml spoons thin honey	4 tablespoons thin honey
1 × 1.25 ml spoon ground cloves	¼ teaspoon ground cloves
900 ml boiling water	1½ pints boiling water
little lemon juice	little lemon juice

Steaming – 15 minutes
L Pressure – 30 minutes OR
H Pressure – 20 minutes

METHOD
Sift the flour and salt into a mixing bowl, stir in the suet and sugar. Gradually add sufficient water until a smooth, elastic dough is formed which leaves the sides of the bowl cleanly.

Turn out on to a floured surface and knead lightly. Take two-thirds of the pastry and roll out into a round, large enough to line a 900 ml/1½ pint pudding basin. Grease the basin with a little butter or margarine and line with the pastry. Pack half the apples into the basin, add half the honey and a little ground cloves. Fill with the remaining apples, honey and cloves in the same order. Roll out the remaining pastry to form a lid, wet the edges and seal over the top of the filling. Cover with a double thickness of greased greaseproof paper or a piece of greased aluminium foil and tie down.

Have the water and lemon juice boiling in the cooker and add the trivet, rim side down. Stand the pudding on the trivet, close the cooker and steam gently, without the weights, for 15 minutes. Raise the heat, bring to L or H pressure and cook for 30 or 20 minutes accordingly. Reduce the pressure slowly. Turn out on to a warmed dish and serve.

Date and orange pudding

METRIC	IMPERIAL
75 g self-raising flour	3 oz self-raising flour
pinch of salt	pinch of salt
75 g fresh white breadcrumbs	3 oz fresh white breadcrumbs
75 g shredded beef suet	3 oz shredded beef suet
50 g brown sugar	2 oz brown sugar
1 × 5 ml spoon mixed spice	1 teaspoon mixed spice
100 g chopped dates	4 oz chopped dates
grated rind and juice of 2 oranges	grated rind and juice of 2 oranges
1 egg	1 egg
a little milk	a little milk
little butter or margarine for greasing	little butter or margarine for greasing
900 ml boiling water	1½ pints boiling water
little lemon juice	little lemon juice

Steaming – 15 minutes
L Pressure – 40 minutes OR
H Pressure – 30 minutes

METHOD
Sift the flour and salt into a mixing bowl. Add the breadcrumbs, suet, sugar, mixed spice, dates and orange rind. Mix thoroughly. Beat the orange juice and egg together. Stir into the dry ingredients with sufficient milk to form a mixture with a soft dropping consistency. Grease a 900 ml/ 1½ pint pudding basin with a little butter or margarine and place the mixture in the basin. Cover with a double thickness of greased greaseproof paper or a piece of greased aluminium foil and tie down. Have the water and lemon juice boiling in the cooker and add the trivet, rim side down. Stand the pudding on the trivet. Close the cooker and steam gently, without the weights, for 15 minutes. Raise the heat, bring to L or H pressure and cook for 40 or 30 minutes accordingly. Reduce the pressure slowly.

Apple and honey pudding

Blackcurrant roly poly

<table>
<tr><td>METRIC</td><td>IMPERIAL</td></tr>
<tr><td>225 g self-raising flour</td><td>8 oz self-raising flour</td></tr>
<tr><td>pinch of salt</td><td>pinch of salt</td></tr>
<tr><td>100 g shredded beef suet</td><td>4 oz shredded beef suet</td></tr>
<tr><td>50 g caster sugar</td><td>2 oz caster sugar</td></tr>
<tr><td>150 ml cold water</td><td>¼ pint cold water</td></tr>
<tr><td>1 × 225 g can blackcurrants,
  drained and juice retained</td><td>1 × 8 oz can blackcurrants,
  drained and juice retained</td></tr>
<tr><td>900 ml boiling water</td><td>1½ pints boiling water</td></tr>
<tr><td>little lemon juice</td><td>little lemon juice</td></tr>
</table>

Sauce:

METRIC	IMPERIAL
juice from can of blackcurrants	*juice from can of blackcurrants*
a little water	*a little water*
1 × 15 ml spoon redcurrant jelly	*1 tablespoon redcurrant jelly*
2 × 5 ml spoons cornflour	*2 teaspoons cornflour*

Steaming – 10 minutes
L Pressure – 25 minutes OR
H Pressure – 20 minutes

Blackcurrant roly poly ; Date and orange pudding

METHOD

Sift the flour and salt into a mixing bowl. Stir in the suet and sugar and gradually add the water until a smooth, elastic dough is formed which leaves the sides of the bowl cleanly. Turn out on to a floured board and knead lightly. Roll into an oblong a little narrower than the base of the cooker and approximately 5 mm/¼ inch thick.

Spread the blackcurrants over the pastry to within 1 cm/½ inch of the edges. Damp the edges and roll up, swiss-roll style, sealing all the edges well. Place the roll, with the seam-side underneath, on a greased double thickness of greaseproof paper or a greased piece of aluminium foil. Wrap loosely, making a pleat in the centre to allow for expansion. Secure the greaseproof paper with string at the ends and fold the foil over a few times. Have the water and lemon juice boiling in the cooker and add the trivet, rim side down. Stand the pudding on the trivet, close the cooker and steam for 10 minutes. Bring to L or H pressure and cook for 25 or 20 minutes accordingly. Reduce the pressure slowly.

While the pudding is cooking make the sauce. Make the blackcurrant juice up to 300 ml/½ pint with water. Heat gently in a saucepan with the redcurrant jelly. Blend the cornflour with a little water. Stir into the liquid and bring to the boil, stirring constantly. Slice the pudding and pour the sauce over to serve.

Spotted dog

METRIC

75 g self-raising flour
pinch of salt
75 g fresh white breadcrumbs
75 g shredded beef suet
25 g brown sugar
4 × 15 ml spoons milk
50 g sultanas
25 g currants
25 g chopped mixed peel
900 ml boiling water
little lemon juice

IMPERIAL

3 oz self-raising flour
pinch of salt
3 oz fresh white breadcrumbs
3 oz shredded beef suet
1 oz brown sugar
4 tablespoons milk
2 oz sultanas
1 oz currants
1 oz chopped mixed peel
1½ pints boiling water
little lemon juice

Steaming – 10 minutes
L Pressure – 25 minutes OR
H Pressure – 20 minutes

METHOD

Sift the flour and salt into a mixing bowl. Add the bread-crumbs, suet and sugar. Mix with sufficient milk until a smooth, elastic dough is formed that leaves the sides of the bowl cleanly. Turn out on to a floured board and knead lightly. Roll out into an oblong a little narrower than the base of the cooker and approximately 1 cm/½ inch thick. Spread the fruits and peel over the surface, damp the edges with milk and roll up, swiss-roll style, sealing the edges well. Place, seam-side down, on to a well-greased double thickness of greased greaseproof paper or a large piece of greased aluminium foil. Wrap loosely, making a pleat in the centre to allow for expansion and seal the ends. Have the water and lemon juice boiling in the cooker and add the trivet, rim side down. Place the pudding on the trivet. Close the cooker and steam gently, without the weights, for 10 minutes. Raise the heat, bring to L or H pressure and cook for 25 or 20 minutes accordingly. Reduce the pressure slowly. Turn out to a serving dish and serve with hot custard sauce or slice and serve with butter and brown sugar.

Spotted dog; Toasted coconut pudding; Cinnamon plums with custard sauce

Toasted coconut pudding

METRIC	IMPERIAL
100 g butter or margarine	4 oz butter or margarine
100 g caster sugar	4 oz caster sugar
2 eggs, beaten	2 eggs, beaten
100 g self-raising flour, sifted	4 oz self-raising flour, sifted
50 g desiccated coconut	2 oz desiccated coconut
little butter or margarine for greasing	little butter or margarine for greasing
900 ml boiling water	1½ pints boiling water
little lemon juice	little lemon juice
To finish:	**To finish:**
4 × 15 ml spoons apricot jam	4 tablespoons apricot jam
1 × 5 ml spoon lemon juice	1 teaspoon lemon juice
50 g desiccated coconut	2 oz desiccated coconut

Steaming – 15 minutes
L Pressure – 30 minutes

METHOD

Cream the butter or margarine and sugar until light and fluffy. Beat in the eggs a little at a time. Fold in the flour and coconut. Lightly grease a 900 ml/1½ pint pudding basin with a little butter or margarine. Place the mixture in the basin and cover with a double layer of greased greaseproof paper or a piece of greased aluminium foil, tie down. Have the water and lemon juice boiling in the cooker and add the trivet, rim side down. Stand the pudding on the trivet. Close the cooker and steam, without the weights, for 15 minutes. Raise the heat, bring to L pressure and cook for 30 minutes. Reduce the pressure slowly.

While the pudding is cooking heat the apricot jam and lemon juice in a saucepan. Toast the coconut, on a piece of aluminium foil, under a hot grill. When the pudding is cooked, turn out on to a serving dish and brush liberally with the jam sauce. Sprinkle with the toasted coconut and serve with cream, if liked.

Cinnamon plums with custard sauce

Many of the fruits listed in the fresh fruit chart can be cooked together with a custard. The flavouring or sweetness of the fruit can be adjusted to suit the family's taste. Choose 2 ovenproof dishes that will stand on top of each other without exceeding the two-thirds filling level.

METRIC	IMPERIAL
500 g Victoria plums, stalked and washed	1 lb Victoria plums, stalked and washed
2 × 15 ml spoons brown sugar	2 tablespoons brown sugar
1 × 5 ml spoon ground cinnamon	1 teaspoon ground cinnamon
juice of 1 large orange	juice of 1 large orange
Custard:	**Custard:**
450 ml milk	¾ pint milk
2 large or 3 standard eggs, beaten	2 large or 3 standard eggs, beaten
25 g caster sugar	1 oz caster sugar
little butter or margarine for greasing	little butter or margarine for greasing
a little ground nutmeg	a little ground nutmeg
300 ml water	½ pint water
little lemon juice	little lemon juice

H Pressure – 5 minutes

METHOD

Put the plums into one ovenproof dish. Sprinkle with the brown sugar and cinnamon, mix well to coat the fruit. Add the strained orange juice. Warm the milk to blood heat, pour over the eggs and sugar and beat well. Lightly grease the second ovenproof dish with a little butter or margarine and pour in the strained custard mixture, sprinkle with nutmeg. Put the water and lemon juice into the cooker. Stand the dish of fruit on the base, cover with a piece of greaseproof paper. Add the trivet, to form a shelf, and stand the custard on top, cover this with a double layer of greased greaseproof paper. Close the cooker, bring to H pressure and cook for 5 minutes. Reduce the pressure slowly. Serve the plums with the custard, hot or cold.

Spiced orange bread pudding

A delicious variation of a family favourite.

METRIC	IMPERIAL
6 slices of bread from a large loaf	6 slices of bread from a large loaf
40 g butter	1½ oz butter
2 × 15 ml spoons orange marmalade	2 tablespoons orange marmalade
little butter or margarine for greasing	little butter or margarine for greasing
finely grated rind of 2 oranges	finely grated rind of 2 oranges
a little grated nutmeg	a little grated nutmeg
3 × 15 ml spoons brown sugar	3 tablespoons brown sugar
2 large eggs	2 large eggs
300 ml milk	½ pint milk
300 ml water	½ pint water
little lemon juice	little lemon juice

H Pressure – 5 minutes

METHOD

Remove the crusts from the bread. Spread each slice with some butter and marmalade. Cut each slice diagonally into four. Lightly grease a 1.2 litre/2 pint straight-sided dish that will fit easily into the cooker with a little butter or margarine. Put half the bread slices into the dish, sprinkle with half the orange rind, a little nutmeg and 1 × 15 ml spoon/ 1 tablespoon brown sugar. Repeat this layer with the remaining bread, rind, a little nutmeg and 1 × 15 ml spoon/ 1 tablespoon brown sugar. Beat together the eggs and milk. Strain over the bread and leave to stand for 5 minutes. Press the bread lightly down into the egg and milk mixture. Cover with a double thickness of greased greaseproof paper or a piece of greased aluminium foil. Put the water and lemon juice into the cooker. Add the trivet, rim side down and stand the dish on top. Close the cooker, bring to H pressure and cook for 5 minutes. Reduce the pressure slowly. Lift out and uncover the dish. Sprinkle the top with the remaining sugar, brown and crisp the top under a hot grill.

Rice pudding

METRIC	IMPERIAL
15 g butter	½ oz butter
600 ml milk	1 pint milk
50 g round-grain rice	2 oz round-grain rice
25 g caster sugar	1 oz caster sugar
grated nutmeg	grated nutmeg

H Pressure – 12 minutes

METHOD

Melt the butter in the cooker. Add the milk and bring to the boil. Stir in the rice and reduce the heat so that the milk is at a rolling boil in the cooker. Make sure that the cooker is not more than half full. Close the cooker and, without altering the heat, bring to H pressure. This will take a little longer but will prevent the milk and rice from rising in the pan and blocking the air vent. Cook for 12 minutes and then reduce the pressure slowly. Add the sugar and stir well. Transfer the rice pudding to a lightly greased 600 ml/1 pint pie dish, sprinkle the top with a little grated nutmeg and brown under a hot grill or at the top of a hot oven.

Variation:

Macaroni pudding: can be made in the same way as above, substituting macaroni for the rice. Use 50 g/2 oz macaroni to 600 ml/1 pint of milk. For added richness a beaten egg can be stirred into the cooked pudding before browning the top.

Spiced orange bread pudding

Chocolate pear pudding

Chocolate pear pudding; Rice pudding

METRIC	IMPERIAL
25 g butter	*1 oz butter*
2 × 5 ml spoons ground cinnamon	*2 teaspoons ground cinnamon*
8 glacé cherries	*8 glacé cherries*
2 firm dessert pears, peeled, halved and cored	*2 firm dessert pears, peeled, halved and cored*
100 g butter or margarine	*4 oz butter or margarine*
100 g caster sugar	*4 oz caster sugar*
2 eggs, beaten	*2 eggs, beaten*
75 g self-raising flour	*3 oz self-raising flour*
25 g cocoa powder	*1 oz cocoa powder*
900 ml boiling water	*1½ pints boiling water*
little lemon juice	*little lemon juice*

Steaming – 15 minutes
L Pressure – 30 minutes

METHOD

Melt the butter and pour into a 1.2 litre/2 pint soufflé dish or other suitable size dish. Use a little of the butter to grease the sides of the dish. Sprinkle the cinnamon evenly over the base. Put a cherry into each pear half and place the pears carefully, cut-side down, in the dish. Arrange the remaining cherries between the pears, forming a pattern.

Cream the butter or margarine and sugar until light and fluffy. Beat in the eggs, a little at a time. Fold in the sifted flour and cocoa powder. Spread the mixture carefully over the top of the pears, taking care not to move the pears or cherries and smooth the top. Cover with a double thickness of greased greaseproof paper or a piece of aluminium foil and tie down. Have the water and lemon juice boiling in the cooker and add the trivet, rim side down. Stand the dish on the trivet, close the cooker and steam, without the weights, for 15 minutes. Raise the heat, bring to L pressure and cook for 30 minutes. Reduce the pressure slowly. Turn out on to a warmed serving dish and serve with hot chocolate sauce or whipped double cream.

Coffee rum dessert

METRIC	IMPERIAL
3 large eggs, beaten	3 large eggs, beaten
25 g caster sugar	1 oz caster sugar
1–2 × 15 ml spoons rum	1–2 tablespoons rum
1 × 15 ml spoon instant coffee mixed with 2 × 15 ml spoons hot water, cooled	1 tablespoon instant coffee mixed with 2 tablespoons hot water, cooled
450 ml milk	¾ pint milk
4 × 15 ml spoons single cream	4 tablespoons single cream
little butter or margarine for greasing	little butter or margarine for greasing
300 ml water	½ pint water
little lemon juice	little lemon juice
To finish:	**To finish:**
150 ml fresh double cream, whipped	¼ pint fresh double cream, whipped
1 × 15 ml spoon grated chocolate	1 tablespoon grated chocolate

H Pressure – 5 minutes

METHOD

Beat together the eggs, sugar, rum and coffee. Heat the milk and single cream until blood heat, but do not boil. Pour into the egg mixture and stir well. Lightly grease a 900 ml/1½ pint soufflé dish or straight-sided ovenproof dish that fits easily into the cooker with a little butter or margarine. Strain in the egg mixture. Cover with a double layer of greased greaseproof paper or a piece of greased aluminium foil. Put the water and lemon juice into the cooker and add the trivet, rim side down. Stand the container on the trivet. Close the cooker, bring to H pressure and cook for 5 minutes. Reduce the pressure slowly.

Remove the container and carefully lift off the paper. Leave the dessert to cool thoroughly and chill in the refrigerator for at least one hour before serving. Decorate with rosettes of whipped cream and a sprinkling of grated chocolate to serve.

Brandied pears

This recipe can also be made using fresh peach halves.

METRIC	IMPERIAL
300 ml water	½ pint water
100 g demerara sugar	4 oz demerara sugar
4 dessert pears, a little under-ripe	4 dessert pears, a little under-ripe
To finish:	**To finish:**
4 × 15 ml spoons brandy	4 tablespoons brandy
50 g toasted flaked almonds	2 oz toasted flaked almonds
150 ml double cream, whipped	¼ pint double cream, whipped

H Pressure – 3 minutes

METHOD

Put the water and sugar into the cooker and heat gently until the sugar is dissolved. Peel, halve and core the pears and add to the syrup, coating well. Close the cooker, bring to H pressure and cook for 3 minutes. Reduce pressure quickly. Lift out the pears and transfer to a serving dish. Boil the syrup rapidly until reduced by approximately half. Remove from the heat and cool the syrup slightly before adding the brandy. Pour over the pears and chill thoroughly. Just before serving sprinkle the pears liberally with the toasted almonds and serve with whipped double cream.

Christmas pudding

To allow your pudding to mature and to take advantage of the fresh, new-season fruits, make your Christmas puddings in September or October. This recipe is rich and moist and slices extremely well. Marinating the fruit is not essential but does add to the richness of this traditional recipe. The quantity given below will make 6 individual puddings or 2 × 500 g/1 lb puddings or a 1 × 1 kg/2 lb pudding.

Right: Brandied pears; Christmas pudding; Left: Coffee rum dessert

METRIC	IMPERIAL
175 g stoned raisins	6 oz stoned raisins
175 g sultanas	6 oz sultanas
100 g currants	4 oz currants
2 × 15 ml spoons brandy or rum	2 tablespoons brandy or rum
100 g flour	4 oz flour
1 × 2.5 ml spoon salt	½ teaspoon salt
100 g fresh white breadcrumbs	4 oz fresh white breadcrumbs
100 g shredded beef suet	4 oz shredded beef suet
100 g dark soft brown sugar	4 oz dark soft brown sugar
50 g mixed peel, chopped	2 oz mixed peel, chopped
75 g ground almonds	3 oz ground almonds
50 g glacé cherries, chopped	2 oz glacé cherries, chopped
1 medium cooking apple, peeled and finely chopped	1 medium cooking apple, peeled and finely chopped
1 × 5 ml spoon mixed spice	1 teaspoon mixed spice
finely grated rind and juice of 1 orange	finely grated rind and juice of 1 orange
finely grated rind and juice of 1 lemon	finely grated rind and juice of 1 lemon
2 × 15 ml spoons black treacle	2 tablespoons black treacle
3 large eggs, beaten	3 large eggs, beaten
approx. 300 ml dark ale or stout	approx. ½ pint dark ale or stout

METHOD

Put the raisins, sultanas and currants into a basin, add the brandy or rum and stir well. Cover and leave to marinate for 2 to 3 days, stirring occasionally. Sift the flour and salt into a large bowl, add the breadcrumbs, suet and sugar and stir well. Add all the remaining ingredients including the marinated fruit and its liquid, stir well to combine. The consistency of the pudding should be soft and should drop easily from a spoon. Grease the appropriate basin with a little butter or margarine, see note on Pudding bowls below. Cover the pudding with a double thickness of greased greaseproof paper and a piece of greased aluminium foil or a pudding cloth and tie down with string. Have the required amount of water and a little lemon juice boiling in the cooker. If you have a Hi-dome cooker, the two 500 g/1 lb puddings can be cooked one on top of the other, with the trivet in between. Do ensure that the height of the basins does not obstruct the centre vent. The amount of water required for the large pudding may come over the top of the pudding itself but this will not harm it. Close the cooker and steam the pudding, without the weights, for the required time. Raise the heat, bring to H pressure and cook for the required time. Reduce the pressure slowly. Remove the wet covers, recover with fresh greaseproof paper and store in a cool place.

To reheat the pudding put 900 ml/1½ pints boiling water and a little lemon juice into the cooker. Add the trivet, rim side down. Stand the pudding on the trivet and bring to H pressure. Cook for 10 minutes for the individual puddings, 20 minutes for the 500 g/1 lb puddings and 30 minutes for the 1 kg/2 lb pudding. Reduce the pressure slowly.

Pudding bowls: The individual puddings can be cooked in dariole moulds or small teacups; the 500 g/1 lb puddings should be cooked in 600 ml/1 pint basins and the 1 kg/2 lb pudding should be cooked in a 1.2 litre/2 pint basin.

	WATER FOR COOKER	STEAMING	H PRESSURE
Individual puddings	900 ml/1½ pints	10 minutes	50 minutes
500 g/1 lb puddings	1.25 litres/ 2¼ pints	15 minutes	1¾ hours
1 kg/2 lb puddings	2 litres/3½ pints	30 minutes	3 hours

Apple crunch

Although this recipe uses apples, gooseberries or apricots can be substituted if preferred. It is delicious hot or cold, served with whipped double cream or ice cream.

METRIC

75 g butter

300 g packet half-coated plain chocolate digestive biscuits, crushed

little butter or margarine for greasing

750 g cooking apples, peeled, cored and sliced

finely grated rind and juice of 1 lemon

2 × 15 ml spoons demerara sugar

300 ml water

little lemon juice

IMPERIAL

3 oz butter

10½ oz packet half-coated plain chocolate digestive biscuits, crushed

little butter or margarine for greasing

1½ lb cooking apples, peeled, cored and sliced

finely grated rind and juice of 1 lemon

2 tablespoons demerara sugar

½ pint water

little lemon juice

H Pressure – 7 minutes

METHOD

Melt the butter in a saucepan, stir in the crushed biscuits. Lightly grease a 1.2 litre/2 pint soufflé dish or other suitable size dish with a little butter or margarine. Put a layer of sliced apples over the base, sprinkle with half the lemon rind, half the lemon juice and 1 × 15 ml spoon/1 tablespoon of sugar. Cover with half the biscuit mixture and press down lightly. Repeat with the remaining apples, lemon rind and juice, sugar and crumbs. Cover the dish with a double layer of greased greaseproof paper or a piece of greased aluminium foil and tie down. Put the water and lemon juice into the cooker and add the trivet, rim side down. Stand the dish on the trivet. Close the cooker, bring to H pressure and cook for 7 minutes. Reduce the pressure quickly.

Crème caramel

METRIC

3 × 15 ml spoons granulated sugar

3 × 15 ml spoons water

little butter or margarine for greasing

300 ml milk

150 ml single cream

2 large eggs, beaten

25 g sugar

300 ml water

little lemon juice

IMPERIAL

3 tablespoons granulated sugar

3 tablespoons water

little butter or margarine for greasing

½ pint milk

¼ pint single cream

2 large eggs, beaten

1 oz sugar

½ pint water

little lemon juice

H Pressure – 3 minutes

METHOD

Heat the granulated sugar and water in a small saucepan, without boiling, until the sugar is completely dissolved. Boil rapidly until it caramelizes and is a deep golden colour, take care not to burn the caramel. While making the caramel, lightly grease 4 teacups or dariole moulds with a little butter or margarine. Divide the caramel between the containers. Pour carefully and turn each container, so that the caramel coats the sides and base.

Warm the milk and cream to blood heat, pour over the eggs, add the sugar and stir well. Strain into the containers. Put the water and a little lemon juice into the cooker and add the trivet, rim side down. Stand the containers on the trivet and cover each with a piece of greaseproof paper. Close the cooker, bring to H pressure and cook for 3 minutes. Reduce the pressure slowly. Lift out the crème caramels and chill thoroughly before serving.

Crème caramel; Apple crunch; Right: January fruit salad

January fruit salad

METRIC	IMPERIAL
100 g prunes, stoned	*4 oz prunes, stoned*
100 g dried apple rings	*4 oz dried apple rings*
100 g dried apricots	*4 oz dried apricots*
100 g dried figs	*4 oz dried figs*
600 ml boiling water	*1 pint boiling water*
50 g demerara sugar	*2 oz demerara sugar*
1 × 15 ml spoon honey	*1 tablespoon honey*
1 × 2.5 ml spoon mixed spice	*½ teaspoon mixed spice*
2 oranges	*2 oranges*
50 g whole blanched almonds	*2 oz whole blanched almonds*

H Pressure – 10 minutes

METHOD

Put the prunes, apple rings, apricots and figs into a basin. Cover with the water and a plate and leave to stand for 10 minutes. Transfer the fruit to the cooker with the soaking liquid. Add the sugar, honey, spice and finely grated rind from the oranges. Close the cooker, bring to H pressure and cook for 10 minutes. Reduce the pressure slowly. Transfer to a serving dish and chill thoroughly. Divide the oranges into segments, removing any pith, pips and skin. Stir the orange into the chilled fruits with the almonds. Serve with whipped double cream.

Preserves

If you have never tried to make your own preserves before, do try now that you have a pressure cooker. The time involved is so often the obstacle but, by using the cooker to soften the fruit, a batch of Orange and ginger marmalade for example can be completed in just 1½ hours from start to finish, see page 136.

For the newcomers to preserve making, perhaps it should be explained that the pressure cooker is used only to soften the fruit and extract the pectin. This is usually a very lengthy process and after this is done, the sugar is added and the preserve completed in the open cooker.

Pectin is the natural setting agent obtained from fruits and is contained in varying amounts depending on the fruit itself. Pectin can be destroyed by excessive heat and for this reason it is recommended that fruits are softened using M (10 lb) pressure. Citrus fruits, however, contain high amounts of pectin in their pith and pips and can be softened at H (15 lb) pressure for a slightly shorter time, without harming the pectin.

The amount of liquid used in the pressure cooker is considerably less; approximately half the amount required for the conventional saucepan method. This is because none of the liquid is lost through evaporation during the softening process and, as a result, the preserve will be deliciously full-flavoured.

The boiling times, to achieve setting point, are a little flexible but the time given in each recipe should act as a guide. A sugar thermometer is, of course, extremely useful for this purpose as it eliminates much of the guesswork.

Points to remember for perfect results

1. **Good quality fruit.** The fruit should be only just ripe, never over-ripe and soft. Blemished or bruised fruit should be discarded as these can affect the keeping quality of the preserve. All fruits should be quickly washed and dried *just* before use.
2. **Pectin content.** The setting quality of your preserve depends on the pectin content of the fruit used. Fruits fall into three main groups.

Good Pectin	Medium Pectin	Poor Pectin
Apples	Fresh Apricots	Cherries
Blackcurrants	Blackberries	Marrow
Citrus Fruits	Greengages	Raspberries
Damsons		Rhubarb
Gooseberries		Strawberries
Plums		
Redcurrants		

To ensure the maximum extraction of pectin, acid in the form of lemon juice, citric or tartaric acid, can be added to the fruit. Often a good pectin fruit will be mixed with a poor one to ensure a satisfactory set, e.g. apple and raspberry.

3. **Volume.** The trivet is never used in preserve making and the pressure cooker *must never* be more than half full when the fruit and liquid have been added.
4. **Liquid.** Pressure cooked preserves use approximately half the amount of water required by other methods and this is particularly important to note if you are adapting any of your own recipes.
5. **Reducing pressure.** This may be done by reducing the pressure either quickly or slowly. If reducing pressure quickly, add 2 minutes to the pressure cooking time.
6. **Sugar.** Preserving sugar is the best type to use but loaf or granulated sugar are also quite satisfactory. To ensure that the sugar dissolves quickly and thoroughly it is best to warm the sugar slightly before it is added to the softened fruit. The sugar should be stirred over a low heat until completely dissolved and then boiled rapidly, without stirring, until setting point is reached.
7. **Setting point.** There are three different methods that may be used to determine the setting point:
   a) Put a small amount of the preserve on to a cold saucer and cool. If a skin forms and wrinkles when pushed with a spoon, setting point has been reached.
   b) Take a small amount of the preserve on a wooden spoon. Turn the spoon several times and if the last few drops form as blobs of jelly, setting point has been reached.
   c) Use a sugar thermometer and wait until the temperature reaches 104°C/220°F.
8. **Potting.** All jars must be clean, warmed and dry. Put a metal spoon into each jar as it is filled to absorb the heat of the preserve.
   Marmalades – after setting point has been reached, leave to stand in the cooker for at least 5 minutes until a thin skin forms, then stir well before potting. This ensures that the peel will be evenly distributed throughout and will not rise in the jars.
   Jams and jellies – transfer to their jars immediately, unless they are whole fruit when they should be treated as for marmalades above.
9. **Covering and storing.** Cover immediately with a waxed disc and when cool add a cellophane cover. Label and store in a cool dry place.

Lemon and lime marmalade

Lemon and lime marmalade

Use only ripe limes otherwise the marmalade may be bitter.

METRIC	IMPERIAL
500 g lemons	1 lb lemons
500 g limes	1 lb limes
900 ml water	1½ pints water
2 kg preserving or granulated sugar, warmed	4 lb preserving or granulated sugar, warmed

M Pressure – 10 minutes OR
H Pressure – 8 minutes

METHOD

Wash the fruits well. Using a potato peeler or sharp knife remove the rinds from the fruits and cut into thin strips. Remove all the pith and pips from the fruits and tie them into a piece of clean muslin cloth. Cut the fruits coarsely, saving any juice, and put into the cooker with any fruit juice, 450 ml/¾ pint water and the muslin bag. The cooker should not be more than half full. Close the cooker, bring to M or H pressure for 10 or 8 minutes accordingly. Reduce the pressure quickly. Remove the muslin bag from the cooker and allow to cool slightly. Squeeze the bag over the softened fruit to remove as much juice and pectin as possible and then discard.

Return the open cooker to the heat, add the remaining water and the warmed sugar. Stir over a low heat until the sugar is completely dissolved. Raise the heat and boil rapidly until setting point is reached, approximately 15 to 20 minutes. Skim and allow to stand until a thin skin forms. Ladle into warmed, dry jars. Cover with waxed discs, when cold add cellophane covers and label.

Yield approximately 3 kg/6 lb.

Orange and ginger marmalade

METRIC	IMPERIAL
1 kg Seville oranges	2 lb Seville oranges
juice and pips of 2 lemons	juice and pips of 2 lemons
25 g root ginger, bruised	1 oz root ginger, bruised
1.2 litres water	2 pints water
2 kg preserving or granulated sugar, warmed	4 lb preserving or granulated sugar, warmed
175 g crystallized ginger, finely chopped	6 oz crystallized ginger, finely chopped

M Pressure – 10 minutes OR
H Pressure – 8 minutes

METHOD

Wash the fruit well. Using a potato peeler or sharp knife, remove the rind from the oranges and cut into thin strips or thicker strips if you prefer a coarse-cut marmalade. Halve the oranges, squeeze the juice and remove the pips. Cut the fruit into quarters and remove the pulp. Tie the orange pulp into a piece of clean muslin cloth with the pips from the oranges and lemons and the root ginger. Put 600 ml/1 pint water, the orange and lemon juice, orange peel and muslin bag into the cooker, the cooker should not be more than half full. Close the cooker and bring to M or H pressure for 10 or 8 minutes accordingly. Reduce the pressure quickly. Remove

the muslin bag from the cooker and allow to cool slightly. Squeeze the bag over the cooked peel to remove as much juice and pectin as possible, then discard.

Return the open cooker to the heat, add the remaining water, the warmed sugar and crystallized ginger. Stir over a low heat until the sugar is completely dissolved. Raise the heat and boil rapidly until setting point is reached, approximately 15 minutes. Skim and allow to stand until a thin skin forms. Stir the marmalade before ladling into warmed, dry jars. Cover with waxed discs, when cold add cellophane covers and label.

Yield approximately 3 kg/6 lb.

Grapefruit marmalade

The quantities and method in this recipe can be used exactly to make Seville Orange Marmalade, substituting Seville oranges for the grapefruit.

METRIC	IMPERIAL
1 kg grapefruit, approx. 3	*2 lb grapefruit, approx. 3*
pips and juice of 2 lemons	*pips and juice of 2 lemons*
1.2 litres water	*2 pints water*
2 kg preserving or granulated	*4 lb preserving or granulated*
* sugar, warmed*	* sugar, warmed*

M Pressure – 10 minutes OR
H Pressure – 8 minutes

METHOD

Wash the grapefruit well. Using a potato peeler or sharp knife, remove the rind from the grapefruit and cut into thin strips. Remove all the pith and pips from the grapefruit. Tie the pith and pips in a piece of clean muslin cloth with the lemon pips. Coarsely chop the grapefruit and place in the cooker with the rind, lemon juice, 600 ml/1 pint water and the muslin bag, the cooker should not be more than half full. Close the cooker, bring to M or H pressure for 10 or 8 minutes accordingly. Reduce the pressure quickly. Remove the muslin bag from the cooker and allow to cool slightly. Squeeze the bag over the cooked fruit to remove as much juice and pectin as possible, then discard.

Return the open cooker to the heat, add the remaining water and the warmed sugar. Stir over a low heat until the sugar is completely dissolved. Raise the heat and boil rapidly until setting point is reached, approximately 15 minutes. Skim and allow to stand until a thin skin forms. Ladle into warmed, dry jars. Cover with waxed discs, when cold add cellophane covers and label.

Yield approximately 3 kg/6 lb.

Grapefruit marmalade ; Orange and ginger marmalade

Plum and orange jam

METRIC	IMPERIAL
1 kg plums	2 lb plums
finely grated rind and juice of 2 oranges	finely grated rind and juice of 2 oranges
300 ml water	½ pint water
1 kg preserving or granulated sugar, warmed	2 lb preserving or granulated sugar, warmed

M Pressure – 3 minutes

METHOD

Wash and dry the plums carefully. Cut into halves and remove the stones. Tie the stones into a piece of clean muslin cloth. Put the plums into the cooker with the orange rind and strained juice, muslin bag and water. Close the cooker, and bring to M pressure for 3 minutes. Reduce the pressure slowly. Lift out the muslin bag and discard. Add the warmed sugar and stir over a low heat until the sugar is completely dissolved. Boil rapidly until setting point is reached, approximately 15 to 20 minutes. Transfer to warmed, dry jars. Cover with waxed discs, when cold add cellophane covers and label.

Yield approximately 2 kg/4 lb.

Damson and port wine jam

METRIC	IMPERIAL
1.5 kg damsons	3 lb damsons
300 ml water	½ pint water
4 × 15 ml spoons port	4 tablespoons port
1.5 kg preserving or granulated sugar, warmed	3 lb preserving or granulated sugar, warmed
knob of butter	knob of butter

M Pressure – 5 minutes

METHOD

Wash and dry the fruit and prick each damson with a fork. Put the fruit and water into the cooker. Close the cooker and bring to M pressure for 5 minutes. Reduce the pressure slowly. Add the port and warmed sugar. Stir over a low heat until the sugar is completely dissolved. Boil rapidly until setting point is reached, approximately 15 to 20 minutes. Add a small knob of butter to the jam and stir (this will bring the stones to the surface and they can then be removed with a slotted spoon). Transfer to warmed, dry jars. Cover with waxed discs, when cold add cellophane covers and label.

Yield approximately 2.5 kg/5 lb.

Above: Rhubarb and ginger jam; Left: Plum and orange jam in the pressure cooker; Damson and port wine jam

Rhubarb and ginger jam

METRIC	IMPERIAL
1.5 kg rhubarb, washed and cut into 2.5 cm pieces	3 lb rhubarb, washed and cut into 1 inch pieces
juice of 2 lemons	juice of 2 lemons
25 g root ginger, bruised	1 oz root ginger, bruised
300 ml water	½ pint water
1.5 kg preserving or granulated sugar, warmed	3 lb preserving or granulated sugar, warmed
100 g crystallized ginger, finely chopped	4 oz crystallized ginger, finely chopped

M Pressure – to pressure only

METHOD

Put the rhubarb into the cooker with the strained lemon juice. Put the squeezed lemons and pips into a piece of clean muslin cloth with the ginger, tie securely and add to the fruit with the water. Close the cooker and bring to M pressure only. Reduce the pressure slowly. Remove the muslin bag and discard.

Return the open cooker to the heat, add the warmed sugar and crystallized ginger. Stir over a low heat until the sugar is completely dissolved. Boil rapidly until setting point is reached, approximately 10 minutes. Transfer to warmed, dry jars. Cover with waxed discs, when cold add cellophane covers and label.

Yield approximately 2.5 kg/5 lb.

Bramble jelly

Jellies are made in the same way as jams but instead of the whole fruit in the final result it is only the juice that is used.

Many fruits make good jellies, e.g. apples, blackcurrants, and redcurrants and each of these can be substituted in the recipe below using the same proportions and cooking time. The yield will depend on the amount of juice extracted from the fruit.

METRIC
1.5 kg blackberries, hulled
  and washed
juice of 2 lemons
300 ml water
granulated or preserving
  sugar, warmed

IMPERIAL
3 lb blackberries, hulled and
  washed
juice of 2 lemons
½ pint water
granulated or preserving
  sugar, warmed

M Pressure – 3 minutes

METHOD
Put the blackberries into the cooker together with the strained lemon juice and water. Close the cooker and bring to M pressure for 3 minutes. Reduce the pressure slowly. Press the fruit well with a wooden spoon to extract the maximum amount of juice and pectin then strain through a jelly bag or several thicknesses of muslin. Measure the juice, and add 500 g/1 lb sugar for each 600 ml/1 pint of juice.

Return the juice to the open cooker with the warmed sugar. Stir over a low heat until the sugar is completely dissolved. Boil rapidly until setting point is reached, approximately 15 to 20 minutes. Transfer to warmed, dry jars. Cover with waxed discs, when cold add cellophane covers.

Bramble jelly; Apple and raspberry jam

Apple and raspberry jam

This combination of fruits gives the delicious flavour of raspberries without the enormous cost involved when fresh raspberries are used entirely alone.

METRIC	IMPERIAL
1 kg cooking apples, peeled cored and roughly chopped	*2 lb cooking apples, peeled cored and roughly chopped*
300 ml water	*½ pint water*
500 g raspberries, hulled and cleaned	*1 lb raspberries, hulled and cleaned*
1.5 kg preserving, loaf or granulated sugar, warmed	*3 lb preserving, loaf or granulated sugar, warmed*

M Pressure – 4 minutes

METHOD

Put the prepared apples into the cooker with the water. Tie the apple peel and cores into a piece of clean muslin cloth and add to the fruit. Close the cooker and bring to M pressure for 4 minutes. Reduce the pressure slowly. Lift out the muslin bag and cool slightly. Squeeze the bag well to obtain as much juice and pectin as possible, then discard. Add the raspberries to the cooker.

Return the open cooker to a low heat and stir in the warmed sugar. Stir over a low heat until the sugar is completely dissolved. Boil rapidly until setting point is reached, approximately 15 to 20 minutes. Transfer to warmed, dry jars. Cover with waxed discs, when cold add cellophane covers and label. Store in a cool dry place.

Yield approximately 2.5 kg/5 lb.

Cooked mincemeat

Cooked mincemeat is worthwhile making, particularly if you are able to take advantage of special prices on the fruits. It also has the advantage of keeping extremely well, up to a year, whereas the uncooked variety should be used within a matter of weeks. The following recipe gives a yield of 2 kg/ 4 lb and is the largest amount that should be prepared in the majority of pressure cookers.

METRIC
1 kg cooking apples, peeled, cored and roughly chopped
225 g stoned raisins
225 g currants
225 g mixed peel, chopped
225 g shredded beef suet
1 × 5 ml spoon ground cinnamon
1 × 2.5 ml spoon ground nutmeg
300 ml water
2 × 15 ml spoons brandy (optional)
500 g dark soft brown sugar, warmed

IMPERIAL
2 lb cooking apples, peeled, cored and roughly chopped
8 oz stoned raisins
8 oz currants
8 oz mixed peel, chopped
8 oz shredded beef suet
1 teaspoon ground cinnamon
½ teaspoon ground nutmeg
½ pint water
2 tablespoons brandy (optional)
1 lb dark soft brown sugar, warmed

H Pressure – 5 minutes

METHOD
Put all the ingredients, except the sugar, into the cooker and stir thoroughly. Close the cooker, bring to H pressure and cook for 5 minutes. Reduce the pressure slowly. Add the warmed sugar. Stir over a low heat until the sugar is completely dissolved. Boil rapidly for approximately 15 minutes or until the consistency is thick and syrupy. Transfer to warmed, dry jars. Cover with waxed discs, when cold add cellophane covers and label. Store in a cool dry place.

Yield approximately 2 kg/4 lb.

Lemon curd

METRIC
4 large eggs, beaten
350 g caster sugar
finely grated rind of 3 lemons
3 × 15 ml spoons lemon juice
75 g unsalted butter, cut into small pieces
300 ml water

IMPERIAL
4 large eggs, beaten
12 oz caster sugar
finely grated rind of 3 lemons
3 tablespoons lemon juice
3 oz unsalted butter, cut into small pieces
½ pint water

H Pressure – 15 minutes

METHOD
Strain the eggs into an ovenproof container that will fit easily into the cooker. Stir in the sugar, lemon rind, strained juice and butter. Cover with a double thickness of greased greaseproof paper or a piece of greased aluminium foil. Put the water and the trivet into the cooker. Cut up one of the

leftover lemons and add to the water to prevent discoloring. Stand the container on the trivet. Close the cooker, bring to H pressure and cook for 15 minutes. Reduce the pressure slowly. Stir the lemon curd well, leave to stand for at least 5 minutes, then stir again before pouring into warmed, dry jars. Cover with waxed discs, when cold add cellophane covers or a lid and label.

Yield approximately 750 g/1½ lb.

Lemon curd will only keep for 6 to 8 weeks but it can be frozen. Cool quickly and pour into plastic or waxed tubs, cover and freeze. To serve, thaw at room temperature for 2 to 3 hours.

Cooked mincemeat; Lemon curd

Chutneys

As with making preserves, chutneys, when cooked in the usual way, can take several hours. As you will see from the cooking times in the recipes, making chutney in a pressure cooker is a very speedy process.

It is important not to have the cooker more than half full when all the ingredients have been added. All the chutneys are cooked at High pressure and pressure is reduced quickly. The boiling times, to achieve the thick consistency, are a little flexible but the time given in each recipe should act as a guide. The recipe amounts have been carefully worked out to suit the majority of cookers.

Always bottle the chutney while it is hot, transferring to clean, warmed, dry jars. Cover immediately with waxed discs and when cold, add cellophane jam covers or plastic covers. Metal covers are convenient to use but they must have a protective lacquer or card lining to prevent attack by the vinegar, which will cause corrosion. Always store your chutney in a cool, dry place. They will store for 6 to 12 months.

The yield for each recipe is not very large, so you may like to make two different varieties. As the times involved are so short it is possible to do this in an afternoon or evening session.

Tomato and red pepper chutney

METRIC	IMPERIAL
1 kg ripe tomatoes, skinned and chopped	2 lb ripe tomatoes, skinned and chopped
2 red peppers, cored, seeded and chopped	2 red peppers, cored, seeded and chopped
1 large onion, peeled and coarsely chopped	1 large onion, peeled and coarsely chopped
1 garlic clove, crushed	1 garlic clove, crushed
1 × 5 ml spoon cayenne pepper	1 teaspoon cayenne pepper
a little salt	a little salt
225 g demerara sugar	8 oz demerara sugar
300 ml malt or pickling vinegar	½ pint malt or pickling vinegar

H Pressure – 5 minutes

METHOD
Put all the ingredients into the cooker and stir thoroughly. Close the cooker, bring to H pressure and cook for 5 minutes. Reduce the pressure quickly. Return the open cooker to the heat and boil rapidly until the consistency is thick (this can take from 15 to 30 minutes). Stir occasionally. Transfer to warmed, dry jars. Cover with waxed discs, when cold add cellophane covers and label.

Yield approximately 1.5 kg/3 lb.

Sweet tomato chutney

METRIC	IMPERIAL
1.5 kg ripe tomatoes, skinned and chopped	3 lb ripe tomatoes, skinned and chopped
2 large onions, peeled and chopped	2 large onions, peeled and chopped
2 × 5 ml spoons paprika pepper	2 teaspoons paprika pepper
1 × 5 ml spoon mixed spice	1 teaspoon mixed spice
1 × 5 ml spoon salt	1 teaspoon salt
300 ml spiced vinegar	½ pint spiced vinegar
225 g granulated sugar	8 oz granulated sugar

H Pressure – 5 minutes

METHOD
Put all the ingredients, except the sugar, into the cooker and stir thoroughly. Close the cooker, bring to H pressure and cook for 5 minutes. Reduce the pressure quickly. Add the sugar and stir over a low heat until it is completely dissolved. Raise the heat and cook until the consistency is thick, stirring occasionally (this can take from 15 to 30 minutes). Transfer to warmed, dry jars. Cover with waxed discs, when cold add cellophane covers and label.

Yield approximately 1.5 kg/3 lb.

From left: Tomato and red pepper chutney; Sweet tomato chutney

Mixed fruit chutney

METRIC	IMPERIAL
225 g prunes	8 oz prunes
225 g dried apricots	8 oz dried apricots
boiling water	boiling water
500 g cooking apples, peeled, cored and chopped	1 lb cooking apples, peeled, cored and chopped
225 g stoned raisins, chopped	8 oz stoned raisins, chopped
1 large onion, peeled and coarsely chopped	1 large onion, peeled and coarsely chopped
1 × 5 ml spoon pickling spice, tied in muslin cloth	1 teaspoon pickling spice, tied in muslin cloth
1 × 5 ml spoon ground ginger	1 teaspoon ground ginger
1 × 2.5 ml spoon ground cloves	½ teaspoon ground cloves
grated rind of 1 lemon	grated rind of 1 lemon
225 g soft brown or demerara sugar	8 oz soft brown or demerara sugar
300 ml malt or pickling vinegar	½ pint malt or pickling vinegar
a little salt	a little salt

H Pressure – 10 minutes

METHOD

Put the prunes and apricots into a large basin, cover with boiling water and leave to soak for 10 minutes. Drain, chop the fruits and discard the prune stones. Put the fruits into the cooker with the remaining ingredients. Stir well. Close the cooker, bring to H pressure and cook for 10 minutes. Reduce the pressure quickly. Remove the pickling spice. Return the open cooker to the heat and boil rapidly until the consistency is thick (this can take from 15 to 30 minutes). Transfer to warmed, dry jars. Cover with waxed discs, when cold add cellophane covers and label.

Yield approximately 1.5 kg/3 lb.

Mixed fruit chutney ; Mango chutney

Mango chutney

A favourite accompaniment to curry, this chutney is hot and spicy.

METRIC	IMPERIAL
4 mangoes, a little under-ripe	4 mangoes, a little under-ripe
25 g salt	1 oz salt
450 ml malt vinegar	$\frac{3}{4}$ pint malt vinegar
1 × 5 ml spoon cayenne pepper	1 teaspoon cayenne pepper
15 g root ginger, bruised	$\frac{1}{2}$ oz root ginger, bruised
15 g whole black peppercorns	$\frac{1}{2}$ oz whole black peppercorns
225 g demerara sugar	8 oz demerara sugar

H Pressure – 5 minutes

METHOD

Peel mangoes and slice the flesh away from the core. Discard the core, put the flesh into a bowl and sprinkle with the salt. Cover and leave to stand for several hours or overnight. Drain and rinse well. Put the mangoes, 300 ml/$\frac{1}{2}$ pint of the vinegar and the cayenne pepper into the cooker. Tie the ginger and peppercorns into a piece of clean muslin cloth and add to the cooker. Close the cooker, bring to H pressure and cook for 5 minutes. Reduce pressure quickly. Remove the muslin bag and add the sugar and remaining vinegar to the cooker. Heat over a low heat until the sugar is completely dissolved then cook rapidly until the mixture is thick and syrupy (this can take from 15 to 30 minutes). Transfer to warmed, dry jars. Cover with waxed discs, when cold add cellophane covers and label.

Yield approximately 1 kg/2 lb.

Sweetcorn and pepper relish

This tangy relish goes well with hamburgers or cold meats or can be used as a side dish for a barbecue.

METRIC	IMPERIAL
225 g sweetcorn kernels, (frozen or canned)	8 oz sweetcorn kernels, (frozen or canned)
2 large green peppers, cored, seeded and chopped	2 large green peppers, cored, seeded and chopped
1 onion, peeled and finely chopped	1 onion, peeled and finely chopped
$\frac{1}{2}$ cucumber, peeled and coarsely chopped	$\frac{1}{2}$ cucumber, peeled and coarsely chopped
3 stalks celery, scrubbed and finely chopped	3 stalks celery, scrubbed and finely chopped
4 tomatoes, skinned and chopped	4 tomatoes, skinned and chopped
salt	salt
freshly ground black pepper	freshly ground black pepper
1 × 5 ml spoon ground turmeric	1 teaspoon ground turmeric
100 g demerara sugar	4 oz demerara sugar
300 ml pickling or malt vinegar	$\frac{1}{2}$ pint pickling or malt vinegar

Sweetcorn and pepper relish

H Pressure – 5 minutes

METHOD

Put all the ingredients into the cooker and stir well. Close the cooker, bring to H pressure and cook for 5 minutes. Reduce the pressure quickly. Return the open cooker to the heat and boil rapidly until the consistency is thick, approximately 15 to 20 minutes. Transfer to warmed, dry jars. Cover with waxed discs, when cold add cellophane covers and label. Store in a very cool place or the refrigerator and use within 3 to 4 weeks.

Yield approximately 750 g/$1\frac{1}{2}$ lb.

Fruit Bottling

As you travel around the countryside there is more and more evidence of fresh fruit available for home preservation. Made into a family outing, it doesn't take long to 'pick your own' or, alternatively, take advantage of ready picked fruits at equally attractive low prices.

Fruits preserved in their peak condition make for a delicious variety of puddings and desserts through the long winter months and give a certain sense of achievement when bottled and displayed on the cupboard shelf. However, in order to achieve good keeping qualities the methods used in processing the fruit are important.

Yeast and often moulds are on the surface of all fruits and these need to be effectively destroyed if fruit is to be kept for a period of time. As well, enzymes that are present have to be inactivated so the natural ripening process of the fruit does not continue. If unchecked, these can also cause spoilage of the fruit.

Bottling allows sterilization to take place by heat, and at the same time creates a seal so that other organisms cannot enter the bottle during storage.

Using a pressure cooker for bottling gives a quick and efficient method of heating and sterilizing and depending on the size of the cooker you own, several bottles can be processed at one time.

Temperature and timing are important for too much of either can lead to over-processing and obvious disappointment. Always use L (5 or $7\frac{1}{2}$ lb) pressure, for this gives the most suitable temperature. As the times are often only a minute or two it is not advisable to become distracted with another task!

Important points to remember for fruit bottling

1. **The cooker.** It is advisable to check that the gasket and safety plug are still working efficiently. Leaking will result in pressure lower than anticipated, and in bottling will result in under-processing.

The trivet is always used in the base of the cooker, with the rim side up. This acts as a protective platform between the direct heat of the cooker base and the glass jars.

Use L (5 or $7\frac{1}{2}$ lb) pressure.

Note: If bottling fruit at altitudes of more than 1000 metres/3000 feet above sea level use M (10 lb) pressure instead of L pressure.

2. **The bottles.** These should be perfectly sound and clean. Chips or flaws on the rims of bottles will cause poor seals, and their contents will not keep, or else the bottles will not seal at all wasting time and effort.

Kilner, or similar jars, designed especially for bottling and the high temperatures involved, are the best to use. Jam and other jars can be used but are less reliable with regard to cracking when heated. Jam or other jars are also much more difficult to pack successfully, so if you intend bottling fruit in future years, the initial outlay on the correct jars will not be extravagant.

3. **Seals and covers.** Whether the bottle has a screw-on-band and separate sealing cover, or a clip-on-top with a rubber ring, the sealing cover or rubber ring should not be used more than once, unless you are absolutely certain that they are not faulty. Screw-on-bands should be checked for rusting. If this is overlooked, the bands can prove almost impossible to remove after a period of storage. If a bottle is correctly sealed it isn't necessary to leave the screw band on as the seal is made by the cover. However, it is common practice to leave the screw band on with a little oil or grease on the inner surface to help prevent rusting. This makes it easier to remove the bands when the fruit is required. If using jam jars, special clip-on-tops are available.

4. **The fruit.** Only good quality, unblemished fruit should be used and the fruit should be graded for equal sizing in each bottle. All fruits should be just ripe, except for gooseberries, which need to be bottled when green and hard to prevent over-cooking. Fruits which discolour after peeling, such as apples or pears, should be placed in a brine solution of 1 × 5 ml spoon/1 teaspoon salt to 600 ml/1 pint water. Thoroughly rinse the fruit in cold water just before packing.

Fruits, such as tomatoes or peaches are normally skinned before bottling. This is simply done by plunging the fruit into boiling water for 30 seconds only then placing into cold water. Care should be taken when the fruit is in the boiling water, as a further 30 seconds can begin to cook the outer flesh and make it soft and mushy. Therefore, in subsequent processing the fruit will become overcooked.

Soft fruits, such as strawberries and raspberries,

give better results if they are soaked overnight in a sugar solution before packing. This method improves the colour of the fruit and helps ensure a better pack, as soft fruits shrink considerably and tend to rise in the bottles, however tightly they are packed to begin with.

Hard fruits, such as cooking pears, may not be softened sufficiently during processing. Before packing in the bottles hard fruits should be prepared; place the fruit in the cooker with water, bring to H pressure only and reduce the pressure quickly. Continue with processing in the usual way.

5. **Sugar syrups or brine.** With the exception of tomatoes, all fruits give best results if bottled in a sugar syrup. Water alone may be used but the flavour and appearance are not generally as satisfactory. Tomatoes are either bottled as a solid pack or in brine. For a solid pack add 1 × 5 ml spoon/ 1 teaspoon salt and 1 × 5 ml spoon/1 teaspoon sugar for each 500 g/1 lb fruit used – do not add any liquid. For a brine solution use 1 × 5 ml/1 teaspoon salt to 600 ml/1 pint water.

To improve the acidity of the pack, which is important for tomatoes, a low acid fruit, 1 × 1.25 ml spoon/¼ teaspoon of citric acid or 2 × 5 ml spoons/ 2 teaspoons lemon juice should be added to each 500 g/1 lb jar of tomatoes during the packing.

The strength of a sugar syrup depends on the intended use for the fruit.

A light syrup is suitable for fruit to be used for cooked desserts, such as pies or crumbles. Use 100 g/ 4 oz sugar to 600 ml/1 pint of water.

A heavy syrup is more suitable for fruits that will be served straight from the bottles as a 'dessert' fruit. Use 225 g/8 oz sugar to 600 ml/1 pint water. Granulated or loaf sugar can be used and should be dissolved in the water, then boiled for 1 minute before use. Avoid boiling the syrup for longer as considerable evaporation will result.

6. **Packing the bottles.** Warm the bottles by standing in a bowl of hot water. After packing, replace the bottles in the water so they remain warm for the boiling syrup to be added. While the bottles are being filled, put the cover and rubber rings into a bowl and cover with boiling water. Pack the fruit as tightly as possible into the bottle, remembering that there will always be some shrinkage of the fruit. This is made easier if the bottles are rinsed out with water just before filling, as you can then slide the fruit into place.

Work the fruit in layers. It helps if the centre is filled a little higher than the outsides.

Soft fruits cannot be tightly packed without damaging them, therefore some rising in the bottles is to be expected. After packing, fill the bottles with boiling syrup, leaving at least 5 mm/¼ inch headspace. This is necessary as the fruits will produce some of their own juice during processing and if the bottles are completely filled the excess liquid will boil out and be wasted. As the bottle is filled, twist from side to side to remove the air bubbles.

Wipe the rim of the bottle and apply the cover and screw-on-band or ring and clip-on-top. After screwing the band on, unscrew a quarter turn to allow for expansion on heating.

The bottles are now ready to be processed.

General instructions for bottling and checking seals

1. While packing the bottles put 900 ml/1½ pints water into the cooker with the trivet and bring to the boil. A little lemon juice or vinegar may be added to prevent discoloration of aluminium cookers.
2. Place the covers or rubber rings into a basin and cover with boiling water.
3. Pack the warmed bottles with the prepared fruit, filling right to the top of the bottle.
4. Add the boiling syrup, twisting and tapping the bottle as you do so to release the air bubbles. Fill to within 5 mm/¼ inch of the rim of the bottle.
5. Wipe the neck of the bottle and apply the cover. Adjust a screw-on-band by turning back a quarter turn.
6. Transfer the warm, filled bottles to the boiling water in the cooker. Do not allow the bottles to touch one another or the sides of the cooker.
7. Close the cooker and bring to pressure on a medium heat. Process for the required time, see chart on pages 152, 153, then reduce the pressure slowly. This will take at least 10 minutes.
8. Using a cloth, lift out the jars and stand on a cloth or wooden board. If screw-on-bands are used, screw these down as tightly as possible and re-tighten after 15 minutes. Leave the bottles to cool.
9. Next day check the seals. Remove the screw-on-band or clip-on-top and see if the cover can be lifted off. If a vacuum has formed the cover will hold firmly and the bottle can be stored. If the cover lifts off a seal has not been formed and the fruit will not keep, therefore it is advisable to use the fruit immediately. Re-processing the bottles is not really satisfactory because the fruit will become over softened.
10. Before storing, wash the screw-on-band or clip-on-top, dry thoroughly and rub the band with a little oil or grease before re-applying to the bottle. Label and date each bottle before storing in a cool dark place.

Timetable for bottling fruit

FRUIT	PREPARATION	MINUTES AT L (5 or 7½ lb) PRESSURE
Apples	Peel, core, cut into thick slices or quarters. Hold in a brine solution until ready for packing. Rinse well before packing.	Slices: 1 minute Quarters: 2 minutes
Apricots	Wash. Whole: prick skins once with a fork. Halved: remove stones.	1 minute
Blackberries	Remove stalks, wash quickly and carefully.	1 minute
Cherries	Remove stalks, wash.	1 minute
Currants – black and red	Remove stalks, wash.	1 minute
Damsons	Remove stalks, wash, prick skin once with a fork.	1 minute
Gooseberries	Top and tail, wash.	1 minute
Greengages	Remove stalks, wash, prick skin once with a fork.	1 minute
Loganberries	Remove stalks, wash. Prepare as for raspberries.	3 minutes
Peaches	Cover in boiling water for 30 seconds, plunge into cold water then peel. Cut into halves, remove stone, or slice.	Halved: 3 minutes Sliced: 1 minute
Pears – dessert pears	Peel, core, cut into halves or quarters.	3 minutes
Cooking pears	Prepare as above. Before packing bring to H pressure with 300 ml/½ pint water. Reduce pressure immediately.	3 minutes

Pineapple	Peel, core, remove eyes. Cut into slices or cubes.	3 minutes
Plums	Remove stalks, wash. Whole: prick skins once with a fork. Halved: remove stones.	1 minute
Raspberries	Cover in boiling sugar syrup. Leave overnight before packing. Drain off sugar syrup and re-boil before adding to bottles.	1 minute
Rhubarb	Cut off leaves and base of stem. Cut into lengths to fit the bottle or small pieces. Pack as tightly as possible.	Forced: 1 minute Garden: 2 minutes
Strawberries	As for raspberries.	3 minutes
Tomatoes – in brine	Peel as for peaches. Pack whole or in halves. Cover in brine solution, add 1×1.25 ml spoon/$\frac{1}{4}$ teaspoon citric acid or 2×5 ml spoons/2 teaspoons lemon juice to each 500 g/1 lb bottle.	5 minutes
Tomatoes – solid pack	Peel, pack tightly, sprinkling salt and citric acid between layers. Allow 1×5 ml spoon/ 1 teaspoon salt to each 500 g/ 1 lb bottle and citric acid as for brine pack. Do not add liquid. A little sugar may also be added for flavour, 1×5 ml spoon/ 1 teaspoon sugar to each 500 g/1 lb bottle.	10 minutes
Purée – tomato, apple or apricot	Peel and cut up fruit. Place in cooker with 300 ml/$\frac{1}{2}$ pint water. Pressure cook for 4 minutes. Reduce pressure slowly. Sieve fruit. Re-boil purée before pouring into warmed jars. Leave 1 cm/$\frac{1}{2}$ inch headspace. For sweetened purée add sugar to taste when re-boiled before packing.	Tomato purée: 5 minutes Apple and apricot purée: 3 minutes

Index

Acknowledgments

The publishers would like to thank The Prestige Group Ltd, Tefal Housewares Elaglen Ltd, and Tower Housewares Ltd for supplying pressure cookers for the photography in this book, and the following companies for the loan of accessories: Craftsmen Potters, Dickins and Jones, Leon Jaeggi, and Liberty & Co Ltd.

Photography: Melvin Grey 14–15, 30–31, 42–43, 54–119, 148–153; Barry Jell 2–5, 16–17, 120, 134–135; Roger Phillips 6–9, 19–29, 32–41, 46–53, 122–133, 136–137

Additional Recipes

Additional Recipes

Additional Recipes

Additional Recipes